THE TURTLE TATTOO

The TURTLE TATTOO

MARGARET OLIVIA WOLFSON

Timeless Tales for Finding and Fulfilling Your Dreams

NATARAJ
PUBLISHING
Mill Valley, CA

Published by: Nataraj Publishing, P.O. Box 2430, Mill Valley, CA 94942

Edited by Hal Zina Bennett; Cover and interior design by Angela Werneke
Illustrations © 1996 by Angela Werneke; Typography by TBH Typecast, Inc.

The author of this book does not dispense medical advice or prescribe the use of any technique as a form of treatment for physical or medical problems without the advice of a physician, either directly or indirectly. In the event you use any of the information in this book, neither the author nor the publisher can assume any responsibility for your actions. The intent of the author is only to offer information of a general nature to help you in your quest for personal growth.

Library of Congress Cataloging-in-Publication Data

Wolfson, Margaret, 1953-
    The turtle tattoo : timeless tales for finding and fulfilling your
dreams / Margaret Olivia Wolfson.
        p.   cm.
    Includes bibliographical references.
    ISBN 1-882591-28-3 (cloth)
    1. Religious fiction, American. 2. Fables, American. I. Title.
PS3573.O56163T87   1996
813'.54—dc20
                                   96-1933
                                    CIP

ISBN 1-882591-28-3

Printed in the U.S.A.

10 9 8 7 6 5 4 3 2 1

First Printing, April 1996

*Dedicated to my dearest parents
who have unfailingly provided my life's ship with
a bright, warm harbor of love.*

CONTENTS

ACKNOWLEDGMENTS

I am indebted to Shakti Gawain and Jim Burns for creating Nataraj, an extraordinary publishing company with a broad and humane vision. It is an honor to be associated with such a first-rate publishing house. Thank you, too, Shakti, for your many wise and subtle suggestions. And hats off to the amazing Jane Hogan, Nataraj's tireless and enormously talented president. Jane, I deeply appreciate the care that you have given this book. I am sure that you must do a juggling act every day to meet the thousand and one demands of publishing, and as far as I'm concerned you've never dropped a ball! Bravo!

I also offer my gratitude to Hal Zina Bennett for his magnificent editorial counsel. I feel unbelievably lucky to have had such an artistic, psychologically astute, wide-souled, rich-minded, word-wizard of a human being for an editor.

In addition, I would like to extend sincere thanks to the hard-working staff at Nataraj—Uma Ergil, Theresa Nelson, Kathy Altman, Susan Ward, and Lynn Johnston for shepherding this book through the publishing maze. And special thanks to Angela Werneke for her inspired and beautiful cover and interior design, and to TBH Typecast for such fine work.

I also wish to express appreciation to all the dedicated people at Hay House—Louise Hay, Reid Tracy, Jill Kramer, Christy Allison, Kristina Queen, and Jeannie Liberati—whose efforts enabled this book to reach the reading public. And a special thanks to Trace Murphy and Jeff Herman for words of encouragement in the book's early stages.

I also want to extend my very deep appreciation to Paula for her unshakable belief in this project—even in its rawest stages—and to Mim, Lena, Alexandra, Nica, George, Inez, Amy, Patti, Marooti, and Tessa for their careful readings of the manuscript. Thank you all for your marvelous feedback and encouragement. You inspired me to do better!

My gratitude also goes out to Mandy—my lighthouse—and to Barbara, Isha, Maxine, and Nabila for reminding me of my strength in a dark time. I am also indebted to Toni, Marlene, Connie, and Mildred for providing me with living examples of courage. And thank you, Buelah, for being the inspiration behind Chapter Eight.

Finally, love and thanks to Cliff, my life partner, artistic colleague, and 24-hour computer hotline. Thank you dearest Cliff for being there throughout this long and difficult journey.

When inspired by a grand purpose,
a wonderful project, your thoughts shatter their bonds;
your mind travels beyond limitations;
your consciousness extends in all directions;
and you discover a new and amazing world.
Hidden forces, talents and faculties spring to life
and you find yourself to be far greater
than you ever dreamed you could be.

Patanjali

PREFACE

The title of this book was inspired by an ancient Chinese fairy tale. In that story, a young man performs an act of compassion, and as a reward he receives a gift from a magical being. This gift, a tattoo in the shape of a turtle, causes the earth to become transparent. Suddenly, the man is able to see shining piles of gold and silver beneath his feet—heaps of treasure long buried and forgotten. I like to think of this book as a kind of turtle tattoo. It is my belief that its insights will bring gold into your life—the splendid treasure that awaits all those who fulfill the dreams that mirror their life purpose.

To realize our dreams, we must operate by some basic principles. Throughout the ages, these principles have been presented in many of the world's best myths and folktales, fairy tales, legends, and parables. As a professional storyteller and educator who has spent thirteen years navigating the ocean of story, seeking tales that instruct in the ways of the world and the ways of the soul, I have netted many shining examples.

For several reasons, myths and mythic tales are excellent vehicles for communicating what we must do to realize our dreams. First and foremost, the accomplishment of difficult, soul-enriching dreams and tasks is the theme around which many of these ancient tales revolve. Climbing the slopes of a glass mountain to release a suffering captive or voyaging through the smoking gloom of the Underworld in search of a lost lover, is characteristic of the amazing feats performed by the heroes and heroines of the world's mythic tales. Unquestionably, these stories have a great deal to tell us about what must be done to complete seemingly impossible tasks. When viewed metaphorically, they teach us how to spin the straw of our dreams into the gold of reality.

These tales are also inspirational in nature. The miraculous transformations so many of them describe—penniless beggars becoming kings and queens, mere mortals changing into gods and goddesses—symbolize our ability to break free from limitations and deliver ourselves to a richer, fuller life. And because these tales teach in the mysterious picture-language of the soul, we easily absorb their message. It is not a coincidence that the world's greatest teachers—the Buddha, Moses, and Jesus—as well as shamans and other visionaries of traditional cultures, have used metaphorical and symbolic tales to impart their messages. As an ancient Hebrew proverb has it: "Give people facts and you light up their minds, but tell them a tale and you illumine their souls."

Regardless of your race, religion, or gender, the ideas in this book can help you realize your dreams, especially if you have the good fortune of living in one of the world's free and developed nations. Unlike many countries, in which the soil created by the collective mind may be inhospitable to such an undertaking, the world's free nations provide extremely fertile ground.

The opening two chapters of this book should be read prior to the others and in sequence. The first chapter discusses the importance of uncovering your life purpose. The second chapter explores the vital role thought and belief play in turning dreams into reality. While the last chapter should be read after completing all the others, the remaining chapters need not be read in order. For the most part, the attitudes and practices that help us realize our dreams are like the threads of a tapestry; they are not arranged in hierarchical order, and each attitude or practice, though part of a whole, also stands alone. On page 121, you will also find a brief summary of the eleven dream-realizing principles described in this book. Refer to this list often; it will help you stay the course.

Although the stories in this book retain their ancient narrative structures, each one has been refashioned in my own language. And though I chose stories from a range of traditions, I made no effort to evenly reflect the world's cultures. Rather, I chose stories on the basis of my own personal taste and for how well I felt each tale expressed a specific dream-realizing principle.

Throughout, I touch on the psychospiritual truths contained in the tales. For example, while the folktale about the woman and the tiger in Chapter Two is used to illustrate the roles that persistence and goalsetting play in accomplishing our dreams, it also teaches us about the healing that occurs when we confront and integrate our "tiger"—our Shadow—the dark, repressed, or disowned aspects of self. Perhaps it is simplest to think of these mythic tales as kaleido-scopes—with each turn of imagination's hand, a different aspect of truth reveals itself.

There is a belief in many spiritual and mystical traditions that each human being has been given a special gift by the Creator. This gift is our life purpose, our treasure, and it is mirrored in our deepest dreams. When we dare to bring this gift into the world, we cannot help but flourish. And when one person prospers, many benefit. Just as a single pebble makes ever-expanding rings when striking still water, the accomplishments of one individual ripple out into the world. It is my hope that the wisdom contained in this book will help you realize your dreams, and that those dreams bring riches into your life, and into the lives of those around you.

If there is righteousness in the heart,
there will be beauty in the character;
If there be beauty in the character,
there will be harmony in the home;
If there is harmony in the home,
there will be order in the nation;
If there be order in the nation,
there will be peace in the world.

Confucius

INTRODUCTION

Sometime prior to writing this book, I was feeling out-of-sorts a good deal of the time, and despite the fact that I enjoyed an abundance of blessings, dissatisfaction paced like a caged panther in my soul. I felt frustrated and stressed and had come to see the days of my life not as precious gifts, but as ordeals to be endured. I was, in the words of poet Gerard Manley Hopkins, "Haggard at the heart, care-coiled, care-killed, fagged, fashed, cogged, and cumbered."

Recognizing that such feelings were symptomatic of a deeper problem, I began searching for the source of my discontent. Though I had recently turned forty, I did not believe that emerging wrinkles, slackening flesh, and a loudly ticking biological clock were solely responsible for my malaise. The tragedies of our time, as pictured on television and in newspapers, and viewed daily on the city streets I walked, stirred my compassion, and though powerfully contributing to my feeling that all was not right with the world, I could not truthfully say that these events were the sole cause of the maelstrom in my spirit.

Telling myself that I was fortunate—that I enjoyed excellent health, family, and friends, decent living quarters, and professional success—did little to assuage my feelings of discontent. Nor could I blame my unhappiness on my childhood. I had grown up in a safe and secure neighborhood with two parents who, though excessively worried and anxious much of the time, were nonetheless loving, dependable, and unstintingly generous. Summer nights were not spent in sweltering, bare-bulbed rooms, but outdoors, catching fireflies twinkling above wide lawns. Winter did not bring a misery of unheated rooms and rattling windows, but sun-cracked crystals glittering from eaves. Nor did comparing my situation to that of my ancestors—people who had trekked through Middle Eastern deserts, European ghettos, and the equivalent of American sweat-shops in search of the blessings I enjoyed daily—quell the discontent in my soul.

After considerable reflection, I concluded that my less than happy condition issued from the fact that I was no longer fully living my life purpose—a purpose that demanded I provide myself and others with spiritual refreshment and life-transforming wisdom by artistically capturing and sharing the beauty, truth, and mystery of the world.

True, my work as a storyteller and educator partially expressed this mission, but in addition to performing and teaching, I had been feeling, for a good many years, a strong desire to write a book that more fully explored the psychological, spiritual, and moral dimensions of mythic tales, particularly in the light of Jungian and Transpersonal Psychology. And yet I could not seem to find the time; my need for a dependable income compelled me to fill my calendar with too many professional engagements, many of which were only indirectly related to my purpose. It seemed that my soul, too long denied the opportunity of addressing all aspects of its duty, was finally rebelling.

After much reflection, I came to the conclusion that if I were ever to completely fulfill my mission in life, I would have to break from my present pattern of working. It was clear that I could no longer halfway honor my soul's needs. And though I understood that a change in attitude could transform a less than perfect situation into a tolerable one, I was also familiar with the danger inherent in living a life or doing work that does not fulfill one's deepest needs. Thus, I made a dramatic decision. For a period of six months, I would stop all performing, teaching, and consulting, live on my meager savings, and devote myself to writing the book I had been dreaming of writing for so long.

Although I had not exactly defined the focus of the book, I knew I wanted to present a wealth of spiritual and psychological insight mined from the world's mythic tales. I was not a mythological fundamentalist, believing every myth to be a mother lode of wisdom. Yet I did feel that many of these ancient stories contained priceless gems that, if properly cut, could enrich contemporary living.

Thinking that the soothing world of nature would make an excellent midwife, I began searching for a house in the country. Providentially, I found an odd little house that despite of its uniqueness, did not exceed my price range. Not only did it have a crooked fairy tale turret, but it was surrounded by open fields of wild grass. It also boasted a dark green pond that shone by day like an emerald mirror and sang at night with the passion of bullfrogs. So, with the bullfrogs, an occasional deer, and numerous cups of coffee as companions, I happily settled down to the task of writing.

But as the months passed, my happiness waned. I felt that my writing consisted of little more than esoteric ramblings that popped like shiny bubbles when touched by intellect's sharp fingers. I became aware of the absence of a unifying theme; simply presenting the life-transforming wisdom contained in ancient tales was too broad a task. Frustration deepened when, try as I might, I could not find a theme that would link together all the ancient gems I was mining. Filled with doubt, my productivity plummeted, and before long, I stopped writing altogether. I was in despair when I realized I had no idea of how to bring my dream of writing a book to fruition.

Certainly I had accomplished a deep dream before—that of becoming a professional storyteller—but I had little memory of how I had gone about achieving this success. At that time, I must have intuitively known what to do. But now I was stuck. I longed for some advice that would free me and get me moving again in the direction of my dream.

Searching for answers, I put my writing aside and embarked on an enormous reading project, ferreting out every book written on the subject of realizing personal and professional dreams. I visited bookstore after bookstore, relentlessly searching for principles and practices that, if applied, would help me complete my dream of writing a book and getting it published.

Soon the house was overflowing with books drawn from a variety of disciplines—literature, psychology, consciousness, metaphysics, religion, and motivational training. I read day and night in cafes and restaurants, in the quiet of the house and outdoors beneath the trees, encouraged by the industrious ants scurrying across my page.

Then, one night, several months after I had been into this reading project, I had a dream. It was an amazing dream, a big dream, a dream so timely and perfect that it seemed like a heavenly gift. In this dream, I was giving a storytelling concert for an adult audience. I was telling the story mentioned in the preface of this book, the story of turtle tattoo. As I was speaking, the stage, like the earth in the tale, suddenly became transparent, and piles of gold and silver glittered just beneath my feet.

When I awoke, I felt the currents of certainty coursing through my body. The hopelessness I had been feeling was gone. The dream had revealed the theme of my book; it had given me the thread that would link all the sparkling stones I had been gathering together. I now understood that my task was to illumine, through the use of mythic tales, the success principles I had been painstakingly gathering all summer. Unlike the vast majority of self-help books that simply *told* people how to accomplish a dream, it occurred to me that a storytelling approach would *show* them in a colorful, moving, and inspiring way.

Two months after this enlightening dream, the time came for me to leave my mountain home. I remember gazing out the sliding glass doors. From time to time, I heard the delicate splash and plop of turtles, as they left their rocks and dove into the emerald pond, the water rings widening in their wake. A pair of butterflies floated by, and a dragonfly sparkled past the window.

Watching this beautiful scene, I felt wistful. Like the paired butterflies fluttering in the late September light, my days in this lovely landscape were also numbered. Before long, I would be back in the din of New York, the gentle sounds of birdsong and insect buzzing replaced by the clang and clatter of the city. Melancholy overcame me as I realized I would no longer be able to watch the wind send shudders of silver across the grass, nor thrill to the sight of the blue loon, sweeping low across the pond. There was no question about it; I simply was not ready to return. Yet my reluctance to leave did not really matter. What mattered was this: I now knew with absolute certainty what I had to do to realize my dream.

Throughout the difficult task of writing, rewriting, and editing this book, and then during the arduous job of finding a publisher who shared my vision, the principles I have written about sustained me. Each time I had doubts or ran into obstacles, the stories themselves—sometimes one, sometimes several—helped carry me through.

Knowing, as you do now, that the book you are reading is the product of the tools it talks about, let it be the inspiration and proof you need to convince you that by following its guidance, you too can make your dreams come true.

*To know rather consists of
opening out a way whence the
imprisoned splendor may escape
than in effecting entry for
a light supposed to be without.*

Robert Browning

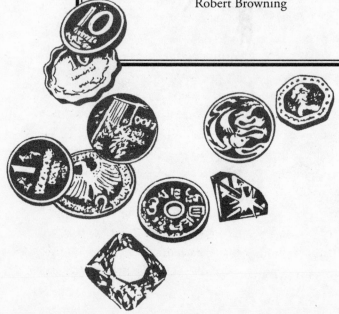

CHAPTER ONE

THE SPLENDOR WITHIN
✦DISCOVERING YOUR PURPOSE ✦

When we live in accordance with our divinely decreed purpose, we experience a deep and lasting contentment. The way we fulfill and express this divinely decreed purpose is through actualizing our dearest aspirations, our innermost dreams. These dreams can be likened to the colored glass cups that hold votive candles. When the light of purpose shines through the glass of our dreams, radiant color streams into the world.

If we truly want to transform our lives, we must discover our life's purpose, the splendor within. Without an understanding of our purpose, it is difficult to distinguish between dreams spun from the shining sands of the soul's need from those blown of false, unhealthy, or fleeting desire. Accomplishing the latter may bring financial gain or momentary pleasure, but such achievements will not fill our lives, and by extension, the lives of our communities and world, with the all-suffusing glow of spiritual and emotional well-being. As eloquently expressed in the Bible: "What shall it profit a man, if in gaining the whole world he loses his soul?"

It is one of the tragedies in growing up that so little time is given to the study of purpose. "What do you want to do when you grow up?" is a perfunctory question we adults often ask children, particularly when we can't think of anything else to say. Because our educational system pays scant attention to the development of purpose, most of us grow up with little understanding of the splendor locked within ourselves. Just as Aladdin, the hero in that mystical old story, *Aladdin and the Wonderful Lamp,* failed to understand that the transparent fruits hanging on the trees in the underground cave were really gems of inestimable value, we too often fail to see the value of our inner treasure—our life purpose.

Unfortunately, it often takes a life-threatening illness or other traumatic event to awaken many of us to the importance of uncovering and then fulfilling our life purpose. This was poignantly revealed to me during a series of storytelling and writing workshops that I was conducting for a women's group of recovering substance abusers who were also HIV positive.

Although much of the unhappiness experienced by these women is rooted in childhoods tortured by the triple-headed demon of abuse, poverty, and familial addictions, an exercise that we did once revealed a surprising fact: many of these women identified feelings of purposelessness as the primary source of their misery. When struck by the chilling reality of AIDS, many of these women experienced an overwhelming desire to finally discover and begin living their purpose. Not coincidentally, those who remained healthiest were the ones who had discovered and begun expressing the splendor within.

Fortunately, it is not necessary to have a serious illness to awaken to the importance of finding and expressing our life purpose. If you haven't yet uncovered this treasure, the following story, from *A Thousand and One Nights,* that rich collection of tales passed from one generation to the next by Arabian, Persian, Indian, and Jewish storytellers, tells us where to look.

≋

Long ago, in the ancient city of Baghdad, there lived a wealthy merchant named Hamid. Hamid owned the most beautiful villa in the city, and his garden was a sight to behold. Waist-high roses flanked the pathways, and in the garden's center stood a fountain made of dark golden stone. Hamid often relaxed near this fountain; he loved listening to the splash and tinkle of its cascading, crystal-clear waters.

But one day Calamity—that awful worm in the rose, that serpent in the grass—struck with unrelenting force, and Hamid was left completely destitute. He had to sell his house and was forced to eke out a miserable existence by begging. Now the sad owner of a tiny cup, the once rich Hamid pleaded daily with the indifference of strangers. His ears, once entertained by the soothing sound of falling waters, were now assaulted by the hard plink! plink! of pity's coins striking metal. His nose, formerly host to the perfume of roses, grew accustomed to the smell of poverty—the rotten odor of crushed hope.

One night Hamid had a dream. In this dream, a voice told him to go to Cairo, for there he would find his fortune. And so, when Hamid awoke, he set off for that distant city.

He traveled dusty roads and walked through scorching deserts. He passed tiny villages and bustling towns. Finally, after many days and nights, he reached Cairo. Because he had no money for lodgings, he huddled up in the mosque's courtyard, seeking a few hours' rest.

As he was sleeping, a thief broke into a house adjacent to the mosque. Hearing the robber, the owners shouted for the police. Within moments, the police arrived, but they were too late; the thief had already escaped. Swinging their clubs, the officers combed the neighborhood, searching for

the burglar. Soon they discovered the hapless Hamid, asleep in the courtyard of the mosque. Believing him to be the thief, they hauled him off to
prison. After a day and a night had passed, Hamid was released from his
tiny cell and brought before a judge.

"Where are you from?" the judge asked.

"Baghdad," Hamid answered.

"And what are you doing in Cairo?"

"In Baghdad I had a dream, and in this dream a disembodied voice
told me that on waking, I should set off for Cairo to claim the fortune
awaiting me there."

Hearing these words, the judge scoffed at Hamid, "Why, only a
fool travels from one country to another because of a dream! I too had
a dream, and in my dream a voice said, 'Awake and go to Baghdad!
When you arrive, seek out the most splendid villa in the city. Go to
that villa, and in its garden you will see a fountain. Dig your way to
the fountain's center, and there you'll find a trunk filled with priceless
gems and gold.' But do you think I went to Baghdad because of a
dream? Of course not!"

The judge handed Hamid some money and told him to return to
Baghdad. Full of hope, he began the long journey home.

When he reached his former house, Hamid went straightaway to the
fountain and began digging in the earth. And though his muddy hands
ached from their work in the chilly soil, he did not lessen his furious
efforts.

After several hours, he felt something hard. He dug some more and
soon uncovered an antique trunk. He pulled it out of the earth, he lifted
the lid, and a dazzling sight greeted his eyes. The trunk was brimming
with jewels and golden treasure! His wealth restored, Hamid lived out
the rest of his days in peace and prosperity.

To learn from this tale, we must read it symbolically. It is not a story about overland travel or the discovery of physical treasure; rather, it teaches that our own backyard is the place we must look when life has lost its richness. If we unearth the treasure buried deep within our beings, we will be able to throw away the tin cup of lack and live with greater abundance.

When we find this treasure—our life's true purpose—and begin actualizing that purpose in the world, we experience a rush of vibrant energy. This energy is like the crystal-clear water of a fountain that refreshes and renews. To find this treasure, we must dig deeply into the loam of our passions.

One way you can begin digging for your purpose is by making a list—over a period of several weeks or so—of everything that moves, excites, or inspires you. For example, a list I once made over a three-week period included the following:

1. Hearing a dove singing on a sun-splashed, leaf-shadowed morning

2. Crafting a metaphor that, like a magic mirror, made the invisible visible

3. Watching a wheel of pigeons flash pink and white in the sky

4. Smelling the earthiness of spring mud

5. Exchanging smiles with a passing stranger

6. Experiencing a transcendent moment while performing

7. Working on a story and finding just the right words to describe a scene or character

8. Watching an insecure workshop participant gain confidence through the act of developing and telling her life story

9. Witnessing the pleasure on the face of a depressed friend after being introduced to a spiritually uplifting and psychologically illuminative poem

10. Performing stories for handicapped children and watching their awestruck faces as they imaginatively voyaged to new and distant worlds

After you have made your list, note the main theme or themes running through your entries. In my case, three themes dominated. One reflected my deep connection to the mystery and beauty of the world (1, 3, 4, 5). Another theme revealed my love and fascination with the artistic process (2, 6, and 7). The third reflected the deep pleasure I receive from helping people break free from their limitations (8, 9, and 10).

Once you have identified the major themes running through your entries, weave them into a single statement that very broadly describes your aim and how you will accomplish that aim. For example, when I did this, I deduced that my life purpose was *to help people transform their lives by calling their attention to the mystery, truth, and magic of the world through the vehicles of dramatic performing and writing.*

After you have identified your life purpose, make a list of your dreams. Write down everything you have ever wanted to do, be, or have. After you have created this list, check each dream against your life purpose. Those dreams that are powerfully linked to your life purpose, either directly or indirectly, are the ones worth pursuing. As you struggle to turn these dreams into reality, you will be provided with many challenges and exercises that will contribute to your spiritual and emotional development.

You will also discover that the dreams that are most closely aligned with your life purpose are the ones that you already have at least some ability for realizing. Dreams that express your life's true purpose are never unattainable—they are decidedly within your grasp. The gold of purpose is always contained within a treasure trunk crafted from our personal skills and aptitude.

Some years ago, a newly divorced, somewhat melancholy man named David attended a storywriting workshop I was giving for teachers in the Catskills. The goal of this workshop was to show participants how stories could be used as tools to help students envision the futures they wanted. To reach this goal, I asked each member of the group to write a story that embodied what they considered their life purpose.

To get the participants started, I suggested that they give their main characters a vocational purpose. David responded by saying that he could not think of a vocational purpose for his character, probably because he never had one for himself. He had only become a teacher because he wasn't sure what else to do.

The next day, David came to the workshop with his young son Peter. During the workshop, David entertained Peter by carving a small block of wood. As chips and curls fell to the floor, a horse with a flowing mane and delicately notched hooves gradually emerged. At some point in the workshop, David was asked to describe his talents. In spite of the miracle taking shape under his artful carving, he claimed that he had no talent. I then asked him what he loved above all in life, and he quickly responded, "Working with wood and making children happy."

After he articulated his passion, the group began to discuss various ways that he could wed his carpentry skills to his passion. As a result of this discussion, David finally found a vocation for his fictional character. His hero became a maker of toys who, in the manner of the playthings in Hans Christian Anderson's fairy tale, the *Tin Soldier,* came alive at night. In his story, wooden cars zipped about the living room, and wooden animals stalked their prey, all under the watchful eye of a small boy.

Several years after this workshop, I received a letter from David. A year earlier, he had opened up a little shop and was now making wooden playthings. He was also exhibiting his works at trade and craft shows, and taking orders at the New York Toy Fair. In addition, he was delivering talks to children in schools and hospitals on the art of making high-quality wooden toys. On top of this professional success, his personal life had taken a turn for the better— soon he was planning to remarry.

If we don't understand our life purpose, we run the risk of becoming ambulance chasers—running after ideas that, at best, bring momentary financial gain. This can be seen in the case of a close friend of mine who, like many in midlife, is not completely at peace with her life's circumstances. In quest of a more prosperous existence, she has been spending considerable time dreaming up off-beat mechanical inventions.

Secrecy forbids me from sharing these inventions with you, but I can say this: although many of her ideas are very clever, I do not believe she will devote the time and energy necessary to develop and market them. Without exception, all of them are too far removed from her genuine passion, which is expressed through her musical talent and ability to help people, particularly children, unlock their joy with the key of sound.

None of the mechanical inventions that her mind so easily constructs are related to her passion. Because she never becomes deeply invested in the process of crafting these mechanical inventions into reality, she will never have access to the soul-force required to carry something from initial stage to final completion.

Once on the path to realizing our innermost dreams—the ones that embody our divinely appointed purpose—our lives undergo an amazing transformation. Feelings of darkness, heaviness, and isolation begin to disappear. Of course, living our purpose doesn't mean an end to life's difficulties and obstacles, setbacks and pain—for in truth these are the crucibles in which our souls are forged—yet it does promise that we will be better able to handle such events when they happen. Like Hamid, we, too, can become rich in so many ways when we unearth and use the treasure buried in our own backyard—our divine gift, our purpose, our reason for being.

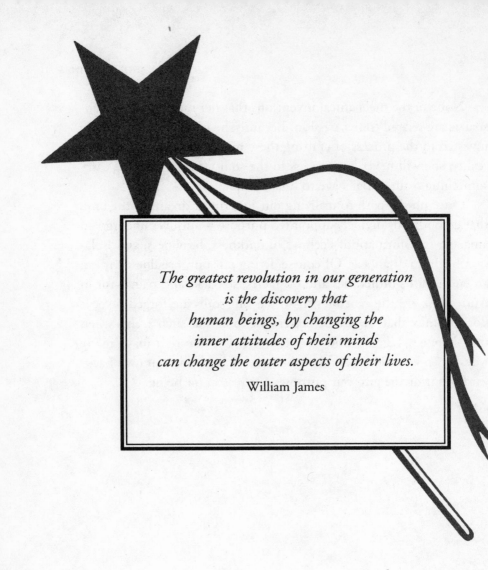

The greatest revolution in our generation
is the discovery that
human beings, by changing the
inner attitudes of their minds
can change the outer aspects of their lives.

William James

CHAPTER TWO

THE MAGIC WAND
•THOUGHT AND BELIEF•

As a child, I was fascinated by magic wands. And so, when the air grew cold and Halloween pumpkins glowed hot and orange on stoops, I eagerly opened the box containing my favorite costume—a store-bought rendition of a fairy's gown. But it wasn't the robe that intrigued me. My imagination was sparked by the stick with the star on its end. It did not matter that this wand was nothing more than cardboard, glue, and silver glitter. I believed it possessed amazing power; with a simple wave it could make physical objects appear and disappear.

Like this magic wand, our thoughts and beliefs have the power to create or transform the outer aspects of our lives. This is partially because our beliefs and thoughts determine the choices we make—both consciously and unconsciously—and the manner in which we respond to life's events. Reality is not a mute stone existing independently of us somewhere "out there," but a soft clay modeled by our expectations.

Although not omnipotent, beliefs (emotionally charged thoughts) and thoughts (ideas about things) do create, to a significant degree, our outer circumstances. While there is much in the world that is out of our control—as an old African proverb has it, you cannot use your hand to force the sun to set—many ancient creation stories suggest that mental activity gave rise to reality or at the very least, breathed life into its inert forms.

In the Egyptian creation myth, for instance, the Creator wrote the world into existence with a reed pen, and in the Biblical story, Divine Intelligence brought the universe into being with a series of commands. These commands, in turn, brought forth light and darkness, the seas and dry land, grass and fruit-yielding trees, whales and winged fowl, beasts and fish of every kind, and the first human being.

In the creation myth of the Hopi Indians, Spiderwoman sculpted birds and fish, animals and trees, bushes, plants, and human figures out of soft clay. She covered these shapes with her white blanket, and swaying her gleaming bronze body back and forth, sang the Song of Creation. When she lifted the white blanket, the power of her song had transformed the motionless clay figures into living things. The creation story of the Australian aborigines also describes how the world was sung into existence.

In the Mayan creation story, the thoughts of Maker, Feathered Serpent, and Heart of Heaven blend together and cause the waters to recede and earth to appear. Mountains and valleys, trees and flowers, roaring thunder and zigzagging lightning, deer and birds, pumas, jaguars, and snakes all spring from the mingled thoughts of Maker, Feathered Serpent, and Heart of Heaven.

In the ancient creation story of the Persians, Ahura Mazda, the deity of supreme light, is birthed from the thoughts of Zurvan, the Creator. But then Zurvan undergoes a period of doubt, and from these dark thoughts, Ahriman, the god of evil, is born. Like these powerful myths, the charming story below, a Zen teaching tale from Japan, clearly illustrates how our thoughts and beliefs help create our physical reality.

There once was a man named Tsuge who loved to visit his dear friend, Atsuko. Atsuko was a gracious hostess, and whenever Tsuge came over she gave him a cup of delicious green tea. Tsuge sipped his tea slowly as he shared the news of the day with Atsuko. He always left her house feeling relaxed and refreshed.

But one day, to his horror and astonishment, Tsuge saw a tiny snake wiggling at the bottom of his teacup. Not wanting to embarrass his hostess, he said nothing. Instead, he drank his tea quickly and pushed away his cup. He talked a bit more, but suddenly feeling sick, he excused himself and returned home.

That night, Tsuge had terrible cramps in his stomach. He shook and trembled, sometimes hot and sometimes cold. His legs stiffened and his head ached. There was no doubt in his mind—he had been poisoned by the snake in his tea. Tsuge became so ill he believed he might die. He called the local healer, who asked him many questions and examined him carefully, but could find nothing physically wrong. Still, Tsuge's discomfort continued to rob him of his sleep. When he was able to doze, he was plagued with dreams of his impending death.

When Atsuko heard of her friend's illness and its cause, she was horrified and rushed to his side, insisting that he come to stay with her so that she might nurse him back to health. Tsuge accepted and went to her home.

When they arrived, Atsuko told Tsuge to sit at the table. "I have made you some tea," she said. "It may help soothe your pain." The alarmed Tsuge politely declined her offer, saying he wasn't in the mood for tea, that it would only worsen his condition. But nonetheless, Atsuko placed the steaming cup in front of him, insisting that it would make him feel better. To Tsuge's horror, he saw that a tiny snake was once again wiggling at the bottom of the cup.

Tsuge could remain silent no longer. "My dear Atsuko," he said. "I am grateful for your kindness, and I know you mean no harm by serving me this tea. But I must tell you that the reason I became ill in the first place is because of your tea. When I visited you last, there was a snake at the bottom of my teacup. And I am sorry to say this, but there is a little snake at the bottom of this cup as well."

Atsuko smiled. She then instructed Tsuge to look up. Tsuge did so, and he saw a piece of rope dangling from a beam, twisting back and forth in the breeze. At that moment, he realized that the snake at the bottom of his cup had been nothing more than a reflection in the tea, playing a trick on his mind.

When we recognize that many of the circumstances of our lives are directly or indirectly created by the beliefs and thoughts we hold, we experience a feeling of tremendous liberation. We can hardly deny that social, political, cultural, and/or natural forces can injure innocent people. And surely it would be folly to claim that the victim is always completely responsible for his or her circumstances. Nevertheless, it should be clear to all thinking people that by changing our beliefs and thoughts we can do a great deal to shape the part of our reality that is responsive to our individual will, and that additionally, with right thought and belief, we can transform the negative conditions created by forces beyond our control.

Although our personal power is not unlimited, the idea that our inner attitudes can change our external circumstances, gives cause for celebration. Destiny is not a fixed entity, but rather a fluid condition created by the ongoing interaction between our internal and external worlds. As human beings, we are co-creators, and as such, possess tremendous power to construct the circumstances of our lives. As the new physics is revealing and as many of the world's ancient myths tell, ours is a participatory universe.

It is not an easy task to identify the beliefs and thoughts in our minds. Very simply, the mind can be compared to a glacier; the tip can be thought of as the conscious mind, and the submerged mass below can be likened to the subconscious or personal unconscious. Stored in this region are all the experiences and perceptions of our individual lives, both positive and negative. Over time, these experiences and perceptions crystallize into various thoughts and beliefs.

The ocean surrounding this glacier is analogous to the Universal Mind, or what psychologist Carl Jung called the collective unconscious. Found in this ancient sea are all the experiences and images of humankind, indeed of all life itself. The place where our personal unconscious and collective unconscious meet is our supraconscious or higher unconscious. It is perhaps simplest to refer to this extraordinary part of our being as our Higher Self.

Roberto Assagioli, the founder of psychosynthesis, a transpersonal or spiritual psychology, describes the supraconscious or the Higher Self, as the place where "we receive our higher intuitions and inspirations—artistic, philosophical, or scientific, ethical 'imperatives' and urges to humanitarian and heroic action. It is the source of the higher feelings, such as altruistic love; of genius and of the states of contemplation, illumination, and ecstasy. In this realm are latent the high psychic functions and spiritual energies."

We often experience our Higher Self in the form of our instincts and intuitions—our "gut level" response to things. We can also draw wisdom from our Higher Self by silently posing questions, and then patiently waiting for answers. However, when performing this simple exercise, be wary of instructions that encourage you to think or act in ways that might bring harm to yourself or others. This sort of information flows from the less developed part of your personal unconscious. Information gleaned from the Higher Self is always ethically, morally, and spiritually sound, and fills you with hope and a desire to perform beneficial and life-affirming actions.

Undeniably then, our unconscious mind is a mighty reservoir of powerful wisdom. But, as we have seen, the unconscious also contains thoughts and beliefs that do not always serve us well. Becoming aware of these hidden *negative* thoughts and beliefs is critical, for more than anything else, they have the power to sink the ship of our dreams.

At one time while writing this book, I experienced a prolonged period of writer's block. Using the simple exercise mentioned above, I uncovered the belief that was causing this problem. I repeatedly asked myself what could be inhibiting the flow of my ideas. Then using paper, pens, a computer, and collage materials, I recorded whatever spontaneously arose in my mind in words, thoughts, or pictures. To tease this inner material to the surface, I tried not to judge or edit the responses that came up, even if at first they did not appear related to my question.

By the end of the week, I examined the responses I had gathered and discovered that part of my writer's block was due to a hidden belief that females are incapable of creative acts. I believe that this idea took shape during my formative years because that was a time in our history when virtually all significant accomplishments were attributed to males. Rockets shot to the moon, bridges spanned rivers, books rolled from presses, and factories churned out goods because of men, not women. Television and primary school readers provided images of high-heeled women dusting immaculate houses, and throughout most of my teen years, the literature and art I was exposed to was largely the creation of men.

Prior to this discovery, I was not aware that I held such limiting beliefs. Despite my 1950s childhood, I saw myself as a product of the feminist movement. During my college years, I awoke to the idea that women could accomplish whatever they desired. And yet, apparently the old belief was still lingering deep within me. When I finally uncovered this hidden belief, it lost some of its power. Under the gaze of conscious observation, I began to feel this dream-sinking belief melt away—releasing me from my creative block.

Here is another example: I know a man, whom I will call Joseph, who, for many years, has been stuck in a low-level managerial position that makes little use of his formidable abilities and talents. Because of this he is deeply frustrated, debt-ridden, and in poor physical health. Unfortunately, Joseph *unconsciously* contributed to the creation of these life conditions.

Despite the fact that Joseph was clear about his life purpose, he was always thwarted when he tried to realize the dreams that expressed that purpose. Perhaps this is because, as he asserted many times, he associates power with the oppression of others. Since oppression of others is something he vehemently wants to avoid, it seems clear that for Joseph this belief is a dream-killing poison.

Like most deeply held beliefs, this attitude took root in his childhood. On many occasions, Joseph described the oppression he felt from a domineering and successful father. Because of this, one of his greatest fears was that should he become successful and powerful, he ran the risk of becoming an oppressor, like his father.

In addition to this belief, Joseph expressed another belief that kept him from realizing his dreams or goals. Often he stressed the importance "of looking ahead to avoid potentially dangerous and explosive situations." On the surface, this seems a prudent idea. Yet on closer inspection, we see that this belief focuses on negatives; for Joseph the future is something laden with potential *dangers* and *catastrophes* rather than challenges to be met and overcome.

In and of itself, foresight is an excellent tool, but when it is beaten into a sword designed to ward off the monsters of lurking dangers, it inhibits us from taking the movement necessary to actualize a dream. As such, foresight is no longer a protective saber but a dream-defeating lance. The message communicated by these two examples is clear: you must bring to the surface any thoughts and beliefs that inhibit you from actualizing your dreams, and then replace these thoughts and beliefs with consciously created messages that support you during your dream-realizing quest.

One way to do this is to vividly visualize and affirm your aim over an extended period of time (see Chapters Six and Seven). By doing this, you condition yourself to produce the results you desire. Like Spiderwoman's Song of Creation, carefully crafted thoughts and beliefs can help you breathe life into the clay of your dreams. And, just as the Egyptian God wrote the world into being with a reed pen, the thoughts and beliefs you hold help create the story of your life—a story that, though marked by dark and painful passages that you may never be able to fully transcend or transmute, can still describe, in chapter after chapter, the passion and joy that comes from living your deepest dreams.

*Though you grow
weary from repeated failure,
begin your undertakings again and again,
for fortune smiles
on the one who perseveres.*

Hindu saying

CHAPTER THREE

PATHWAY TO THE TIGER
•PERSISTENCE AND GOALSETTING •

*P*icture a typical schoolday sometime during the 1950s. The smells of textbooks and manila paper, pencils and crayons fill the air, and from the cafeteria, the odor of Sloppy Joes makes its way down the light green cinderblock hallways. On the window sill, the little shoots of the new potato plants are struggling for life in milk cartons.

Because it is storytime, the teacher asks us to come to the corner of the room, and in the culturally insensitive lingo of the time, instructs us to sit "Indian-style." She then takes out a book from a disorderly stack on a blond wood shelf. The book's cover shows us a red steam engine, a smile on its face and a cloud of smoke pouring from its stack.

Like millions of schoolchildren of this era, I often heard the story of *The Little Engine That Could.* In captivating rhythm—*I think I can, I think I can, I think, I think, I think I can!*—this tale described one tiny train's upward struggle. By keeping its goal in mind—getting to the top of the hill—and by persisting in the direction of that goal, the little engine finally accomplishes its dream.

As an adult, one of my favorite poems that speaks about the value of goalsetting and persistence is by the African-American poet, Langston Hughes.

Mother to Son

Well, son, I'll tell you:
Life for me ain't been no crystal stair.
It's had tacks in it,
And splinters,
And boards torn up,
And places with no carpet on the floor-
Bare,
But all the time
I'se been a-climbin' on,
And reachin' landin's,
And turnin' corners,
And sometimes going in the dark
Where there ain't been no light.
So boy, don't you turn back.
Don't you set down on the steps
'Cause you finds it's kinder hard.
Don't you fall now—
For I'se still goin', honey,
I'se still climbin',
And life for me ain't been no crystal stair.

Our goals are like the steps on a staircase—each one leads to the uppermost landing of our dream. The truth is that many of us don't reach our dreams because we don't keep climbing. We expect our staircases to be made of crystal. We expect the "going to be smooth."

When we encounter "tacks and splinters," and "boards torn up," we "sit down on the steps." To realize a dream, we must move relentlessly toward it, no matter what or who tries to stop us. When we find boards torn up, persistence requires that we get out a hammer and nail them down, and when we walk on bare, uncarpeted floors, persistence demands that we take out the wax and start polishing until the dull wood darkly gleams.

The need for persistence is humorously demonstrated in this anecdote concerning a disciple and his master. The disciple asks the master if enlightenment is as bright as one hundred light bulbs. The master replies: "No, much brighter." The disciple proceeds to question the master, each time incrementally increasing the number of light bulbs. Finally, after many months, the weary disciple asks if enlightenment is as bright as one billion light bulbs. To this the master replies, "Brighter." Exasperated, the disciple shouts, "I give up!" Hearing these words, the master replies, "Why? You were getting so close!"

Of course, there are always times in our lives when we feel like quitting. It is during these times that, if we keep persistently completing one goal and then another, until we can, literally, do no more, that our reward will come. As noted by the mythologist Joseph Campbell, "One thing that comes out in myths is that at the bottom of the abyss comes the voice of salvation. The blackest moment is the moment when the real message of transformation is going to come. At the darkest moment comes the light."

Throughout most of your dream-realizing quest, persistence is what will carry you through these dark times, although considerably later in your dream-realizing journey, a time will come when letting go of a goal proves wiser. At the moment of surrender, the light shines through, and suddenly, all you have worked for miraculously appears. We will be exploring this further in the pages ahead. However, for now, let us stay focused on the value of persistence. Without it we will never reach the stage when letting go of our desire releases us into the full realization of our dream.

I distinctly remember the time when I first heard the voice of persistence. About ten years ago I was living in a quiet Brooklyn neighborhood. One chilly autumn evening I was walking home from a long and tiring subway ride. As usual, the neighborhood was deserted and quiet, just the rattling of dry leaves and the yowling of wild cats.

As I passed by the long golden windows of the brownstones flanking the sidewalk, I remembered a scene from Marcel Carne's film *Les Enfant du Paradis (The Children of Paradise)*. In this scene, an extraordinarily gifted but impoverished mime is walking through a lamplit neighborhood. As he passes the long, elegant windows of a Parisian townhouse, he sees a ball going on, and against the lace curtains he sees the whirling shadows of dancers. In a vain effort to be part of this world of lightness and laughter, he begins dancing in the cold streets.

Like the mime in this film, I too was keenly aware of the contrast between my life and what I imagined to be the life behind those long, golden windows, that world of warmth and safety. And so, as the cold wind steadily blew and the dry brown leaves scuttled across the sidewalk, I remember thinking: "How in the world did I end up like this? How did I end up living on the wrong side of the golden windows?"

That night I couldn't sleep. I lay there for hours wondering if life would always be like this—endless subway rides, cold winds, yowling cats, and green-faced clocks ticking out time's passage.

Inside me a hopeless voice repeated itself over and over again: "This is your life and this will always be your life."

But miraculously, I heard another voice that said: "If you want to change your life, you can. If you want the long, golden windows of home or anything else, just determine exactly what it is you dream of accomplishing, chart a course, and keep moving in the direction of that dream." Fortunately, I listened to the second voice. I also got a quartz clock and moved back to Manhattan!

Fairytales abound with examples of how a dream is realized through a character's persistent attempts to realize a goal. These old, magical tales teach us that even when mistakes are made, having goals and persisting until we accomplish them, leads to success. One of my favorite heroes of Russian folktales is Prince Ivan, who makes numerous errors as he seeks the Firebird, the mysterious, flaming bird that nightly steals golden apples from his father's tree. Despite his mistakes, Ivan keeps going, speeding toward the completion of his dream on the back of the Gray Wolf, emblem of endurance.

When trekking towards a dream, we need the endurance of a wolf. The habit of persistence toughens up our souls so that when we step on the thorns and shards of disappointment—which always litters the road to a dream—we can quickly bind up our wounds and keep moving.

Here is a tale that tells about the healing that can occur when we confront and integrate the dark, disowned aspects of our personality. I tell it here because it also vividly demonstrates the roles that goalsetting and persistence play in realizing our dreams. Variations of this story can be found in many cultures: Asian, African, and Russian. The following version is based on a Korean variation. While performing there some years ago, I met an elderly Korean woman who spoke a little English. When I asked her what she thought the story was about, she replied, "The story about know where you go and keep go . . . keep go!"

There once was a woman who married a farmer whose wife had recently died. The man had an adolescent son. The woman, who had wished for a son all of her life, loved the boy and did everything she could to brighten the dark corners of his young heart. She washed and mended his clothes and made him delicious foods—pickled cabbage and thick, spicy soups. At night, she kept a little lantern burning by his bedside, so should he wake, he would not be met by the fearsome dark. Hoping to distract him from his sorrow, she pointed out the beauties of nature—the Indian ringdoves, camellias, overcup oaks, bellflowers, and snowy chestnut blossoms hanging from boughs. But the boy found no solace in nature's bounty nor in his stepmother's kindness and concern. He yearned for his dead mother, and treated his father's new wife like a stranger. Once, when she reached out to stroke his tear-stained cheeks, he even spat in her face.

The poor woman tried enlisting the help of the boy's father, but the farmer threw up his hands in despair; he had no advice to give. It was then that the woman decided to visit the old monk who lived alone on top of the mountain. The monk was well known among the villagers for his ability to make special healing brews. The woman decided she would ask him to make her a brew that would cause her new son to love her.

It was a long and difficult climb to the monk's hut. Slowly the woman made her way up the mountain. Step by step she trudged up the steep, rocky path. With each passing hour, she grew more and more weary. But she kept going, determined to get the brew. When night came, she briefly rested, but well before dawn she rose and resumed her climbing, moving up the steep incline, never stopping until she reached the monk's hut.

Timidly she knocked on the door, and when the old man answered, she put forth her request. The monk answered, "Yes, I can make such a potion for you, but to do so, I must have the whisker of a tiger. There is one who lives in the cave beyond the river. He is very fierce, but his whiskers are strong and beautiful!"

The woman was stunned. "The whisker of a tiger? How can I possibly get such a thing? I will be killed!"

"If it is so important that the boy love you—bring me the whisker!" the monk exclaimed. With these words, he quietly shut the door. Crestfallen, the woman returned home.

For several days, she thought and thought about how to get the whisker. As she cooked and sewed, hoed and swept, the problem loomed large in her mind. At night she lay awake, gazing out into the darkness, turning ideas over and over in her mind until, at last, she settled on a course of action.

Early the next morning, she set off for the path leading to the tiger's cave. While still a good distance away, she set down a little wooden bowl filled with fresh meat and then hid herself in a clump of nearby bushes. Soon after, the tiger came out of his cave. He ambled down the path, winding his way towards the bowl of meat. When the beast neared the bushes, the woman's blood ran cold and her heart thumped against her ribs. She wanted to run, but she wanted the whisker more. Scarcely breathing, she continued to crouch in the bushes, her fear great, but her love greater.

When the tiger began eating, her terror subsided. The beast made no move toward the bushes, although from time to time he raised his head, warily sniffing the air.

For many months, the woman placed a bowl of food on the path leading to the tiger's cave, each time positioning herself a little closer to the bowl. After many months of doing this, it seemed the tiger had grown accustomed to her odor—he no longer suspiciously sniffed the air.

When a year or so had passed, the woman was able to stand a few feet from the animal. The tiger briefly glanced at her and then, indifferent, returned to his bowl of meat.

Several more months passed, and the woman was now able to stand so close that she could feel the tiger's body heat. And then one day, she drew up her courage, pulled out her scissors, and snipped off a whisker.

"Ah, so you finally got the whisker!" the old monk exclaimed when she returned to his hut, proudly waving the stiff white whisker.

"Yes!" the woman cried. "Now make my curative potion . . . the one that will make my new son love me!"

"But you already have the potion," he answered.

"Whatever do you mean?" she cried, barely able to conceal her anger.

The wise old man replied, "Are you telling me that you can soothe the heart of a savage beast and win its trust, but that you cannot do the same with a human child? Approach your new son in the same way you approached the tiger, and I promise that in time, he will come to trust and love you."

And with these words in her head, the woman returned home, thankful to the old monk of the mountains for giving her the curative brew.

This tale echoes the ancient theme that the curative potion is within us. It teaches that the main ingredients in this brew are to know what we must do to reach our goals and then to persist until we have reached them.

Our goals can be big or small, immediate or long-range. Regardless of their size, a goal is a definite, desired end that gives direction to our lives. When we have meaningful goals, the randomness of life disappears. Paradoxically, when we are engaged in accomplishing future goals, we live more fully in the present. Focusing on a goal stills the self-defeating chatter in our minds. When this chattering is stilled, we are not only better able to savor life's moments, but it is also easier to concentrate on what must be done to achieve our dreams.

This tale also instructs us in the actual art of goalsetting. It tells us that we must have a plan, and then break that plan down into small, manageable steps. To achieve her dream of making her new son love her, the woman believed she needed a curative potion. To get this potion, she needed a tiger's whisker.

Her plan for accomplishing this goal included the following: bringing the tiger a bowl of food on a daily basis and standing at a distance while he ate. As time passed and the tiger grew accustomed to her presence, she would inch her way closer and closer.

To most people, the steps involved in accomplishing a goal seem obvious. Yet it is surprising how many of us pursue our goals in a haphazard way. The most important elements in effective goalsetting are:

- Establish reasonable goals that you can accomplish and make sure these goals are related to your dream (for example, if your dream is to create a newsletter, related goals might be things such as reading every book ever written on writing successful newsletters; talking to other people who have created newsletters; compiling data on your target market, etc.).

• Do not set too many goals at the same time; too many goals create confusion, and confusion dissipates energy.

• Move towards your goal step by step; even accomplishing one small action gives a feeling of control and success.

• Define your goals in concrete terms that can be measured (for example, writing a book is not a measurable goal; whereas establishing the number of pages you intend to write each day is).

Setting goals and persistently going after them is essential for achieving any dream. In the main, far too many dreams go unrealized, not for a lack of talent or ability, but because our goals are unclear and we fail to persist until we reach them. As a mosaic is made from a thousand colored chips, so a dream is reached after taking many tiny steps.

Like the woman in the tale, you must inch your way slowly, patiently, sometimes painfully along the path leading to your dreams. And always, when you push through times of darkness and weariness, a new and magical energy will flow into your life—an energy that gives you the strength to press forward. Persistence requires boldness, courage, and bravery and charges you with the responsibility of looking at setbacks and failures as signs of greater things to come. If you keep going, accomplishing one goal and then another, there is no doubt that one day you will find what you so ardently seek.

*If you keep a green branch in your heart
the singing bird will come.*

Chinese proverb

CHAPTER FOUR

BEYOND THE HORIZON
· FAITH ·

My mind is filled with fond memories of spending Thanksgiving with relatives in Michigan. I loved to sit near the snapping fire, watching my aunt at work on her tapestries. In my mind's eye, I can still see her seated on the sofa, framed by a picture window, beyond which stood a tree, a few remaining leaves rippling on its branches. At her feet were piles of bright yarn and fabric, and as she worked, she listened to piano and violin music—my uncle and cousin practicing for upcoming concerts. Wafting through the air came the delicious smells of simmering stews and baking pies, along with the reassuring sound of familiar footfalls and voices.

Perhaps it is because of this memory that my imagination, always busy weaving analogies, finds deep satisfaction in the image of life as a tapestry in progress. On one side there is a perfect and beautiful design in the making, and on the other, a tangle of jumbled knots and trailing threads. Despite the fact that the latter is the side we most often see, faith tells us that the perfect side does exist, though it is often hidden from view.

If we wish to actualize our dreams, we must have faith; we must trust in an Infinite Power far greater than our finite beings can comprehend. Faith transforms the grit of pain into wisdom's pearls, and though it does not justify or explain the presence of evil, illness, or wrongdoing in the world, it is the balm that soothes and heals the wounds these forces can inflict. Like a magic carpet, faith lifts us from the dark ground of hopelessness, and carries us into wider skies of possibility.

If we don't have faith in our ability to realize a dream, nor faith in the Universe's ardent desire to help us do so, we will never accomplish our goals. We must learn to trust not only ourselves but a power much larger than ourselves; we must learn to believe in an Infinite Intelligence that not only hears, but *longs* to answer our calls.

This power is known by many names: God, Higher or Divine Intelligence, Ultimate or Absolute Reality, Spirit, Atman, Christ, Brahman, Allah, the Tao, the Lord, Deep Mind, Krishna, the Creator, or the Universe, to mention a few. Whatever you choose to call this power, it is the mystery that both surrounds us and is within us, just as the sea surrounds an ice floe, and the ice floe is made up of the sea. The divine is both transcendent and immanent.

In its immanent form, this Great Mystery is revealed in phenomena as common as the slow reddening of apples, the gentle smile of a beloved grandmother, the radiating heat of human touch, the sparkle of stars drifting in deep space, the steam of muffins on cold winter mornings, golden nets of sunlight dancing on water, strokes of genius, acts of kindness, and the magical melodies of birds singing in trees.

This Mystery coaxes flowers to bloom and babies to be born; it lights up the sky and deepens it to darkness; it paints the moon silver and ruffles the sea with foam. Once the mirror of our hearts has been sufficiently polished, we are capable of seeing this Mystery as easily in a pair of laughter-lit eyes as in the drama of a tropical sun setting over an ocean of waving gold.

In its fullest sense, faith is a belief in the Divine Intelligence—both within and outside ourselves—that creates and orchestrates all things. Belief in this Tremendous Mystery shields us against doubt, the force that is always ready to grab our dreams and strangle them in a chokehold of disbelief.

In the Bible, God, angered by the faithlessness of the Children of Israel decrees, "I will hide my face from them, I will see what their end shall be: for they are a very forward generation, children who have no faith." The Israelis are then told that the faithless will be burnt with hunger, devoured with burning heat, and afflicted by the teeth of beasts and the venom of serpents.

The agony created by hunger, heat, and poison in one's veins, is a magnificent metaphor to describe the agony created by a doubting mind. This agony prevents us from acting, and without action, we cannot deliver our dreams; they die, stillborn in the womb of mere wishing. Faith can help get us through those times when we feel trapped, when our lives seem futile and our dreams appear distant, even unreachable.

The difficulty so many of us experience with the notion of faith is that we cannot grasp it with out intellects; in order to receive the gift of faith we must momentarily suspend our intellect. It is impossible to reason our way to faith; attempting to do so is like trying to fill a sieve with water. It is not surprising that the intellect rebels before this thing which, like the wind, cannot be measured, tasted, or touched, this thing that we can only know through its effects in the world around us.

Through faith, miracles do come to pass. Indeed faith is a thing of such astonishing power that, symbolically speaking, a mountain can be moved if a person has faith equal in weight and size to a mustard seed. With faith, that which seems impossible, can come to pass. With faith, we know that whatever good we desire will eventually materialize . . . in some form or another. Thus we are able to positively affirm life, regardless of what it brings. This affirmation not only attracts helpful forces to us, but charges us with the energy we need to keep moving in the direction of our dreams.

The following tale, known throughout South India, humorously illustrates how faith can help us maintain a state of inner balance when we are confronted with difficulties that might otherwise snare us in hopelessness or rage.

There once was a king whose chief minister would respond to every crisis by saying in a calm voice, "This is wonderful, truly wonderful."

Now one day the king was out hunting with this minister. As they were walking through the jungle, the king accidentally stepped on a trap set for unsuspecting animals. The steel jaws gripped his toe, nearly severing it from his foot. The king cried in pain as the minister worked to open the trap. After he freed the king's toe, the minister tore off a piece of his shirt and wound the fabric around the king's wound, all the while gesturing to the injury and saying, "This is wonderful, truly wonderful!"

"How dare you speak of my injury as wonderful!" the king shouted angrily. "Because of your insolence you are dismissed from your post! Return at once to the palace and pack your bags!"

As usual, the minister replied, "This is wonderful, truly wonderful!"

Shortly after the minister left, the king heard a rustling sound among the trees, and before he knew what was happening, a group of wild-looking people sprang out and wrestled him to the ground. They gagged him and bound him and dragged him to their camp. From their leader, the king learned that it was a tribal custom to sacrifice whatever was caught on the first day of the hunt. And so the king was tied to a post and the executioner began walking around him, brandishing his sword and intoning strange syllables. But when he noticed the king's bleeding toe, he suddenly stopped and bellowed, "Where did you get this one? He has been cut before! We cannot sacrifice him! Something that has been cut will not do for our God! Release him at once!

When the king reached the palace, he summoned the minister to his side. He said, "I think I now understand why you said 'this is wonderful, truly wonderful,' when my toe was cut. Because of this injury, my life was spared. But I do not understand why you said 'this is wonderful, truly wonderful,' when I dismissed you from your post. What's so wonderful about losing a valued court position?"

The minister answered, "Good reason exists for all things. Though I could not have known it at the time, your dismissal saved my life. Had you not sent me packing, I too would have been captured. Because my toe wasn't cut, your captors would have made me their sacrifice. When you sent me away, my life was spared! And wouldn't you agree that this is wonderful . . . truly wonderful?"

To me, it is the minister's faith that enables him to accept all of life's events as necessary, even when their meaning is incomprehensible. This belief helps him maintain a state of emotional balance in the face of negative experience. The tale is not suggesting that we adapt an attitude of self-destructive passivity in the face of difficulty. Nor does it imply that we should accept brutality, injustice, and wrongdoing in the world as necessary evils. Rather, this story teaches us that *good can arise from bad*—that we can transcend, transmute, or transform a good deal of human suffering—if we do not allow painful events to undermine our life force, but instead view them as part of a grand, if incomprehensible design.

Such faith-informed thinking and feeling can keep us from getting emotionally mired in strength-sapping rage, hopelessness, and despair. When caught in such traps, it is nearly impossible to summon the strength necessary to try to correct the wrongs of the world. Such immobilization severely impacts on our ability to fulfill our life's mission.

Some time ago, I spent several frightening evenings in the Intensive Care Unit of a hospital, as my father, in the aftermath of an auto accident, struggled for life. With me was a woman named Mary, whose daughter was also in Intensive Care, her vital organs ravaged by illness. Well into her seventies, and obviously of meager financial means, Mary sat quietly day after day, her hands folded in the lap of a faded dress, her thin gray hair matted from its long and heavy leaning against the unwelcoming chrome and vinyl chair. My father pulled through, but Mary's daughter was not to know such a victory. Despite the fact that Mary was stripped to the bone with pain, she remained calm in the face of this overwhelming personal tragedy. "God knows best," she said simply when her daughter was finally released from the violent clutches of illness. "My daughter, she be in a better place now . . . she be singin' with the angels." And Mary rose up on her poor, old, tired feet and walked purposefully toward the business at hand—that of raising four, now motherless, grandchildren.

The ancient Chinese ideogram for the word *crisis* is formed from two written characters. One of these characters represents the concept "danger," and the other "opportunity." From this we understand, as did Mary, the woman in the waiting room, and the minister in the folktale, that opportunity is seeded within every crisis. Faith not only allows us to keep going, but gifts us with the ability to see the opportunity in crisis, the light in the darkness. Faith gives us the strength to keep going in the direction of our dreams, even when our strength has been depleted by wrong turns and endless struggle. And if, for unknown reasons, a dream we passionately desire does not come to pass, faith prevents us from becoming tangled up in knots of bitterness and self-pity; like a knife, it can help us cut through such soul-damaging feelings.

Faith teaches us that nothing in life is meaningless, even though that meaning may be temporarily hidden from our view. With faith, we can re-weave life's frayed rug into a magic carpet of the mind that can lift us into the skies of hope, enabling us to see far into the distance, beyond the limiting horizon.

> *The wind turns a ship*
> *From its direction:*
> *The senses, like wandering winds,*
> *Cause our minds to drift*
> *And turn good judgement from its course.*
>
> Bhagavad Gita

CHAPTER FIVE

CROSSING BUTTERFLY VALLEY
• FOCUS •

*W*hen I was five years old, we lived in Southern California, in a crumbling stucco house on top of a hill surrounded by a decaying lemon orchard. At the bottom of the hill was a sheep farm. I remember those sheep . . . dreamy clouds of dust floating up as they moved, the cold clang of their bells, their noses poking through the wire fence. A profusion of gentians and Queen Anne's lace bordered the fence, and hovering above these flowers were hundreds of butterflies, soft as whispers, fanning their powder-blue wings.

Thoroughly enchanted by these butterflies, I dreamt of capturing enough to fill my room; in flights of fancy I saw my walls transformed into rippling sky blue tapestries. Fortunately, childish greed prevented me from realizing this dream. My hands moved in every direction, snatching at one butterfly and then another. Because the net of my attention was so wide, I never caught a single butterfly, despite the fact that I tried for hours.

Today, I recall that childhood adventure and think of it as a lesson that taught me that persistence *without focus* will never lead to the realization of a dream or goal. We can work and struggle to reach our dream, but unless we keep our inner and outer eyes focused on the countless little goals that move us along in our journey, we have little hope of ever arriving. This important lesson is revealed in countless world myths and tales.

In the Greek myth, *Psyche and Eros,* Psyche must journey through the Underworld to obtain the Box of Beauty. Before setting off on her quest, she is instructed by a Stone Tower—symbol of her far-seeing powers—to hold two barley cakes, one in each hand. These cakes will enable her to successfully pass through the Gates of Hades. Guarding those gates is a three-headed dog named Cerberus. If she throws Cerberus a cake, he will allow her to enter and exit in safety.

The Stone Tower tells Psyche that before coming upon the three-headed dog, she will meet three characters who will plead for her assistance. Despite the satisfaction Psyche may gain from helping them, she is warned against doing so. The tower tells her that they are traps, set by the avenging goddess Aphrodite, designed to make her drop the all-important barley cakes. Should she not pass through the Gates of Hades, Psyche will not be able to petition Queen Persephone for the Box of Beauty—the object she so desperately needs to bring about a reunion with her lost lover, Eros.

Herein lies the lesson: To accomplish our dreams, we must stay focused on those things that lead to our dreams, and shut out those things that distract us. Modern distractions can include excessive television watching, telephone talking, Internet surfing, shopping for unnecessary goods, going down the trail of too many ideas, empty socializing, or tending to others' needs so much that we are no longer tending our own. Certain emotional conditions, such as excessive worry, holding onto anger, and compulsive behaviors, are also distractions. When we are so busy reacting to the world around us, it becomes virtually impossible to focus.

The Buddha defines a person of wisdom as one who joyfully relinquishes smaller pleasures to achieve a greater joy. Our ability to focus is strengthened when we practice this art. Having the discipline to refuse the small pleasures afforded by daily life in favor of the lasting peace and joy that can be obtained when we accomplish our life's deepest dreams, is one of the keys that opens the doors to happiness and prosperity.

I have a friend in her late forties who is a sculptor and a teacher. Although her work has not yet received the critical recognition it merits, her artistic devotion has not flagged. For many years, she has lived in a rent-controlled loft, and though the space is not totally suitable for living, she has never considered increasing her teaching load so she can afford a bigger place.

To devote as much time as possible to her sculpting, she has intentionally kept her teaching hours to a minimum. Concurrently, she has disciplined herself to live on a very restricted income. Unlike many her age, she is not in debt, and her mind is free from the gnawing demons of financial anxiety.

Given the time-intensive nature of her art form, she recognized early on that it would be imperative for her to give up for an unknown period of time, the smaller pleasures of life, if she ever hoped to know the lasting joy of realizing her dream—that of embodying in bronze, metal, resin, and fabric the enigmatic language of the soul. And though many other things have contributed to her happiness, her ability to distinguish between smaller pleasures and lasting joy is unquestionably one of the chief things that has helped her lead a spiritually rich and satisfying life.

The importance that focus plays in realizing our dreams is illustrated in the following story, a tale of the Maidu, a Native American tribe located near the San Francisco Bay.

*O*ne day a woman was in the woods, digging for food. After working for a while, she glanced towards her child, sleeping in a cradle board nearby. As the woman gazed at the child, a butterfly floated into her view. It was an extraordinary creature—unusually large with purple wings and curious white markings. Captivated by its beauty, the woman put down her digging tools and started chasing the butterfly.

She followed it for a long time, but the beautiful creature eluded her grasp. Finally, she gave up and lay down beneath a tree to rest. Soon she fell into a deep sleep.

Hours later, she was awakened by a cool breeze blowing across her face. She sat up and to her surprise saw a man standing next to her. His skin was dark brown, almost violet, and he wore animal skins, pounded soft and white and painted with secret designs. The woman's heart trembled with desire.

"I am the Butterfly Man," he said. "Follow me and I will take you to the Country of the Butterflies. To get there, we must journey through the Valley of the Butterflies. As we travel through this valley, hold tightly to my belt. You must not let go. The only way to do this is to keep your eyes focused on my back at all times. Do you understand?"

The woman nodded, got to her feet, and began following the Butterfly Man, her hand gripping his leather belt. When they reached the valley he had spoken of, the Butterfly Man quickened his step. The woman increased her pace and as instructed, kept her eyes fixed on his back.

But when they were halfway through the valley, she saw a breath-taking sight—a shimmering cloud of butterflies hovered overhead.

"Ignore the butterflies!" the Butterfly Man commanded. "Do not let go of my belt!" But the woman did not follow this command; she longed to catch some of the brilliant creatures, now fluttering around her like so many pieces of broken rainbow. She let go of the Butterfly Man's belt and began grasping at the bright, winged creatures. The Butterfly Man kept moving.

After a few minutes had passed, the woman realized that the Butterfly Man was far ahead of her; she watched as he vanished over the horizon. For a moment she felt scared, but when a spring-green butterfly alighted on her arm, she forgot her fear and the Butterfly Man as well. She wanted the beautiful green creature, and all the other butterflies, too. In mad pursuit, she began leaping and turning, her hungry hands clutching the air. But the woman's efforts proved futile, the butterflies were elusive, impossible to catch. After several days of frantic movement, she collapsed—terribly thirsty, tired, and hungry.

Several times she struggled to her feet, and tried to make her way home, but the valley was too wide. She found herself moving in circles, going nowhere. With each passing day she grew thinner and weaker, and the sun burned her skin. At last, she could walk no longer. She stumbled and fell to the ground. Bruised and bleeding she lay there, until finally she died—all alone in the Valley of the Butterflies.

Clearly the woman in this tale was unable to focus. This inability led to moral irresponsibility and ultimately, to death. In pursuit of her dream, the Maidu woman left her child alone in the woods. In doing this, she committed a grave spiritual error. The beautifully balanced troika of spiritual, emotional, and material prosperity does not come to those who abandon sacred responsibilities. Care of our individual souls is not separate from care of family, community, and the world.

If we wish to turn our dreams into reality, we cannot afford to act blindly. We must stay focused, at all times, on the many small steps leading to that dream. Focusing on these little steps enables us to distinguish between real needs and desires and dream-crushing traps. In her journey through the Underworld, the Greek mythological heroine Psyche is able to distinguish between these two kinds of needs, whereas the woman in this Maidu tale is not.

One of the simplest ways to help yourself stay focused during your dream-realizing quest is to make a list. Your list should describe what activities you hope to accomplish each day, week, and month. Post your list where you can see it and refer to it, and update it often. As you complete an activity, cross it out. In addition to helping you stay on task, this is also a way of acknowledging your accomplishments, and this recognition generates a sense of progress and self-mastery.

This story also teaches us about the value of commitment. Commitment is a mental and spiritual vow that demands we give one hundred percent allegiance to a person, thing, or idea. Commitment and focus are closely linked. When our focus wavers, our commitment also wavers. Just as a single crack in a sheet of glass weakens the whole pane, our commitment is weakened each time we lose our focus. At some point, when we have amassed enough cracks, our commitment shatters and we have little or no hope of fulfilling our dreams.

The writer Goethe had this to say about the value of commitment: "The moment one commits oneself then Providence begins to move. Many things occur that otherwise would not have occurred. A flood of events issues from the commitment, bringing all kinds of favorable and unforeseen episodes, meetings, and physical assistance, which one would never have dreamt possible."

Without focus and commitment, our dreams, like the Butterfly Man in the story, disappear over the horizon, and our souls are left thirsty, tired, and hungry. If left in this condition too long, a part of us eventually dies—alone in the Valley of the Butterflies. But if we keep our focus and commitment, there is every reason to believe that what we now only imagine, will one day become real.

Imagination is more important than knowledge. It is the preview of life's coming attractions.

Albert Einstein

CHAPTER SIX

WEAVING THE DREAM BROCADE
•VISUALIZATION•

Perhaps it was only because I was shorter when I was a child, but it seems that the winters then were much snowier than the winters today. I remember waking up after one great blizzard, rejoicing in the fact that school was closed and a whole day stretched before me—a long flow, uninterrupted by the demands of clocks and bells.

Dressed in red rubber boots, mittens, and a hooded jacket, I waded out, with other such snow-proofed children, into a light-shattered world. Forts were constructed and boulders rolled—great, crunching balls of snow that, when viewed from the side, resembled giant white cinnamon buns.

On one such day, I built an igloo. I worked for most of the day on this smooth, domed dwelling, finishing as the daylight was fading into the magical gray of a winter evening. Sitting cross-legged inside the igloo, eyes closed, I imagined myself an inhabitant of some arctic land. My mind's inner landscape was alive with caribou, dancing Northern lights, and an icy lake, where silver fish flashed beneath the frozen surface.

After some time of such imagining, a curious thing happened. These inner mind pictures proved so powerful that it seemed my outer reality changed—the wind whipped into a harsher blowing, and the temperature sharply plunged. When I emerged from the igloo, I found I was alone. I truly believed I had been transported, through the alchemy of my imagination, to the dark twilight of some distant freezing land.

I trudged across the snowy wastes, and when I reached the icy street, an astonishing sight greeted my eyes. Staring down through the translucent surface, I saw a tiny fish. Transfixed, I watched for a few moments. And then, mysteriously as it had appeared, the creature vanished. This same strange experience of a powerfully built inner picture seeming to materialize in the outer world, occurred in another situation as well.

During the summer of Project Bluebook, the official investigation of the UFO phenomena by the U.S. Air Force, the children in my neighborhood, stirred to action by the media, began building "Martian copters" from cardboard boxes; control panels were made from steel junk garnered from trash bins, and two holes were punched at the bottom of the box to free our legs for running. As we held the boxes up, we moved at top speed, certain the cardboard copters would lift us into flight at any moment.

Once, while trying to accomplish this marvel, I closed my eyes, and while madly dashing through the alleyways, I vividly pictured my box flying. I saw myself sailing several inches above the ground. I held fast to this image, and then a miracle took place—an event I will never forget. For one split second, my feet lifted from the ground and I was airborne! This levitation lasted only long enough for me to wonder if it really happened, and try as I might, I could not repeat this experience.

Although these phenomena were most likely hallucinations created by a child's powerful imagination, I cannot say with absolute certainty that there was not a fish swimming beneath that icy Midwestern street or that the cardboard Martian copter had not, for one split second, lifted from the ground. As an adult, I have either experienced or heard of too many episodes in which mental pictures eventually did take shape in outer reality to unequivocally accept the idea that these miracles were simply a child's fantasy.

Visualization, that is, consciously creating mental images, can be a useful method for realizing dreams. As Dr. Willis Harman, Stanford University professor emeritus of Engineering-Economic Systems, states in his book *Global Mind Change:* "When we establish and affirm an intention or a goal, imagining that it is already so, the unconscious mind is programmed to achieve that goal even in ways which the conscious part of the mind does not plan or understand."

Though it is not known exactly how visualization works, consciously created images apparently settle deep into our subconscious. The subconscious mind accepts whatever orders we give it. Unlike the conscious mind, the subconscious does not try to determine whether ideas are true or false, possible or impossible, good or bad. Like the genie in Aladdin's lamp, the subconscious marches boldly forward to fulfill the commands it is given.

If the positive images planted in our subconscious minds are not undermined by conscious or unconscious negative beliefs and thoughts, and if we support these images with appropriate actions, real miracles—no less amazing than a cardboard box defying gravity or a silver fish swimming beneath the iced surface of a Midwestern street—*can* and *do* happen. The Chinese tale below is one of many mythic stories that illustrate how our mental pictures can take shape in the outer world.

In a certain province of China, a widow lived with her three sons. The widow supported herself and her sons by weaving brocade. Her fabrics, woven of shimmering silken threads, were much admired, and in truth, there were many who thought her images as lovely as the birds, flowers, and animals they represented.

One day the widow went to the market to sell a recently completed brocade. It was a splendid piece of work: a firecracker-red dragon twisted in the sky, and the weaver had made the honeybees so lifelike that one could almost hear the whir of their tiny, transparent wings. Not surprisingly, the brocade sold quickly.

Pleased with her sale, the widow decided to spend the afternoon strolling through the marketplace. The stalls brimmed with colorful food and wares, but it was only when she passed by a small shop, a painted scroll hanging in its window, that she stopped to really look.

The painting in the window showed a blue-roofed mansion, a pair of stone dogs guarding the entrance. Willow trees, bamboo groves, and sparkling lily pools encircled the house, and in the distance, sleek brown cattle and flocks of sheep grazed in the fields. Overhead, a scarlet sun blazed.

The widow stood entranced, her heart pounding with excitement. Everything she had ever dreamed of was pictured in this scroll. She stepped into the shop, and without even bothering to bargain, she purchased the painted scroll, emptying her purse of all the gold she'd newly acquired.

When the widow reached home, she unrolled the scroll on the cottage floor and exclaimed to her sons, "Oh, it would be a dream come true to live in a place like this!"

"Yes, it would," the eldest said. "But it's just that—a dream, and a rather foolish one at that. Remember, mother, we are poor people, and poor people live in thatched cottages, not blue-roofed mansions."

The widow stopped smiling, and tears glistened in her eyes. Seeing her dismay, the youngest son, whose name was Wang, spoke up. "Why don't you weave a brocade of this beautiful picture?" he said. "I know this won't be quite like living in such a place, but it just might be the next best thing."

The widow brightened at Wang's suggestion. She set up her loom and began weaving her dream world. She wove day and night, barely stopping to eat or sleep. Wang watched his mother with pleasure, but as the days dragged into months, his two brothers grew more and more unhappy. Finally, the eldest could contain his anger no longer.

"You do nothing all day but weave, weave, weave!" he snapped. "Months and months have passed, and still you haven't finished. We chop and sell firewood all day long, and yet the pantry remains half empty. It is time you went to market and sold this accursed cloth!"

The middle son nodded in agreement, but Wang protested. "Mother's work isn't finished, and she must not sell it! But don't worry, my brothers. I will make sure we have enough to eat." And true to his word, Wang increased the hours he spent chopping and selling firewood.

After one year of almost ceaseless weaving, the widow's weary eyes began shedding tears. When her tears fell on her shuttle, she wove them into the brocade. Transformed by her passion, they became crystal clear ponds. And when her burning eyes dripped blood, she embroidered these drops into the sun, making its scarlet threads even more luminous than before. At last, after three years had passed, the widow declared her tapestry complete. She removed it from the loom, and spread it across the *floor. She called her three sons to her side, and together they stood, gazing at the magical cloth.*

But suddenly, a gust of wind swept into the cottage. The wind slipped beneath the brocade, lifted it into the air, and whisked it out the open window. The widow and her sons chased after the flying cloth, and watched with dismay as it twirled up, higher and higher into the sky, its gold and silver threads twinkling in the light.

Overwhelmed with grief, the widow collapsed and lay sobbing on the ground. The sons carried their mother back to the cottage and helplessly watched as tears streamed down her wrinkled cheeks.

"Please find the brocade," she begged the eldest. "Without it, I will die."

The eldest son nodded, and after gathering together a small bundle of provisions, he set off in search of the brocade.

After a month of traveling, he came to a small stone house. Sitting in front of the house was an old crone, dressed in a many-colored patched robe, and tethered to a nearby tree stood a stone horse. Glowing gold peaches hung from the tree's boughs, shining like hundreds of little suns.

"Where are you going?" the old crone asked. The eldest son told her the story of the widow's brocade. The old woman replied, "Your mother's tapestry has been stolen by the spirits of Sun Mountain. They love things of beauty, and most likely have taken your mother's work to copy."

"Can you help me get to Sun Mountain?" the eldest son asked.

"Yes, I can, if you are able to follow my instructions."

"What must I do?"

"Knock out your two front teeth. The moment you do this, the stone horse will become a flesh and blood animal. Push your two teeth into its gums, and after it has eaten ten peaches, climb up on its back. Don't worry about directing the horse; it knows the way to Sun Mountain.

But be warned. To reach Sun Mountain you must first pass through a Wall of Fire. As you travel through it, do not utter a word of protest. If you scream or even whimper, you will be reduced to ashes. After you have passed through the Wall of Fire, you will be confronted by the Sea of Ice. Enter this sea, and once in its freezing grip, do not shudder. Control your body. If you so much as quiver, you will sink to the bottom of the sea, never to return."

The eldest son's face paled at the old woman's words.

The crone chuckled and said, "It is clear from your fearful face that you cannot even imagine these trials, let alone actually endure them." She then stepped into her little hut and when she returned, she held a wooden box. "Forget Sun Mountain," she said. "Take this box and go home. It is filled with gold. With this money you will be able to live out the rest of your days in comfort."

Overjoyed by this unexpected turn of events, the eldest son took the box of gold and headed home. But when he came to an attractive village, halfway between his mother's cottage and the old crone's hut, he decided to stay. If he settled here, he would not have to share his newly acquired gold.

When the widow learned of her eldest son's betrayal, she implored her middle son to go in search of the brocade. The middle son packed some provisions, and began walking in the direction of the rising sun. Soon he came to the old crone's hut.

But because he responded to the old woman's instructions in the same fearful fashion as his brother, she dismissed him too with a box of gold. Not wishing to share his treasure, the middle son also settled in a village far from his ancestral home.

More months passed, and lines of worry and pain stretched across the widow's face. She grew so weak she could barely speak. Wang pre-

pared little bowls of rice and meats, and gently urged her to eat. But she could not; her grief was too great. Over and over, she saw the brocade sailing across the sky, sailing away from her, vanishing into the sky, lost forever. "My sons . . . my brocade," she sobbed.

Wang's heart ached for his mother. One day, unable to witness her suffering any longer, he said, "Please mother, do not weep anymore. I am going to find your brocade." The widow touched his hand and smiled.

Wang walked in the direction of the rising sun and soon came to the old crone's house. Here he received the same instructions as his brothers, but unlike them he was not afraid.

He picked up a stone, knocked two teeth from his mouth, and pushed them into the gums of the stone horse. Wang waited while the horse nibbled at the peaches, and when it had eaten ten, he mounted the steed and began galloping in the direction of the rising sun.

Wang rode and rode, never stopping until he reached the Wall of Fire. Its roar sounded in the air, and everywhere the flames flickered like the tongues of angry serpents. The heat was overwhelming, and sweat poured down his brow; he felt as if he were suffocating. Nonetheless, he urged his horse onward and bravely entered the Wall of Fire. Though the crackling flames scorched his skin and the hot air seared his lungs, Wang uttered no sound.

When he emerged from the terrible inferno, the Sea of Ice churned before him. The coldness of the surrounding air sealed his nostrils shut, and his tears froze into tiny crystal tracks. Paying no attention to the danger ahead, Wang urged the horse into the icy waves. Without protest, the horse entered the sea and began swimming through the freezing waves. With each icy blast, Wang clenched his teeth and steeled his nerves.

When he emerged from the Sea of Ice, he saw a majestic sight. Sun Mountain rose up steeply before him. Windflowers danced up and down its sides, and fiery clouds burned and drifted near its peak. Wang tethered his horse to a tree and began his ascent.

When he reached the top of the mountain, he saw a silvery pagoda. He entered, and walked down a long passageway. On either side, carved screens opened onto spacious chambers. Wang saw jade statues, teak-wood tables and chairs, and porcelain vases. Antique scrolls hung in alcoves. He gasped with wonder; never in his life had he seen such a place.

He continued walking until he came to a room at the corridor's end. Beneath a milky white pearl, a group of fairy-like women were working at a huge loom. True to the old woman's words, they were busy copying his mother's brocade.

Wang approached the fairy-like creatures and bowed low before them. In a quiet voice he pleaded for the return of his mother's weaving.

One of the fairy women, who was dressed in a red silk robe, looked at Wang, and touched by his bravery, love, and devotion, said, "By morning we will have finished our work. We will then return the brocade to you. Please allow us this time." Wang agreed and sat down to wait.

When the sun rose in the sky, the women declared their task finished and, as promised, carefully began folding the brocade, preparing it for Wang. But as they were doing so, the red-robed woman suddenly called out for them to stop.

"Our copy is not nearly as beautiful as the original," she said in a sad voice. "And I cannot bear to be separated from this cloth." So saying, she ordered the others to unroll the cloth and hang it on the loom. Wang watched as she then embroidered her likeness into the fabric. When she

had finished, she once again folded the brocade and handed it to him. "Now I will always be a part of the beautiful world created by your mother," she smiled.

Wang bade the spirits of Sun Mountain farewell, and holding the precious brocade close to his heart, he began his slow descent. When he reached the bottom of the mountain, he mounted his horse, and as before, braved the Sea of Ice and Wall of Fire.

After traveling for three days and nights, Wang reached the old woman's house. He removed his two teeth from the horse's gums, and returned them to his own mouth. As the teeth took root, the horse changed back into stone. The old woman smiled at Wang and handed him a pair of deerskin shoes. "These will get you safely back," she said. And shod in the deerskin shoes, Wang ran so quickly that the surrounding landscape blurred into bands of green and gold.

When he reached home, he went directly to his mother's bedside and gently stroked her cheek. Feeling his touch, she opened her eyes, and at the sight of the tapestry, color flooded her cheeks. She fingered the heavenly cloth and strength flowed into her limbs. With Wang's help she climbed out of bed, and together they unrolled the brocade across the cottage's old wooden floor. Its gold and silver threads twinkled in the moonlight.

Suddenly the widow stopped smiling. A wind blew into the cottage, and as before, slipped beneath the fabric and whisked it out the open door. The widow and Wang rushed outside.

But this time, the brocade did not rise up into the heavens. Instead, the fabric settled on the ground and began stretching itself in all directions—north, south, east, and west. Then, as Wang and his mother watched, the brocade burst into life!

The sun rose into the sky and night became day. The mansion became real, as did the flower gardens and crystal ponds. Long-tailed birds sang in the boughs of the willow tree, and sleek brown cattle and flocks of sheep grazed in the distant fields. Everything was exactly as the widow had woven it—except for one thing.

In the center of the garden now stood a woman. Wang recognized her as the spirit from Sun Mountain who, unable to part with the beautiful tapestry, had embroidered her likeness into its fabric. Wang and the spirit woman gazed at each other and, in that moment, love stitched itself on their hearts.

Soon news of the widow's miracle spread near and far. The widow invited everyone from miles around to come and share her wealth, a wealth that soon included a pair of persimmon-cheeked grandchildren. And so it was that the old widow lived with her youngest son, his wife, and her grandchildren in a beautiful world that had once been nothing more than a vision in her mind.

One evening, many years later, two beggars passed the mansion. Peering through the gates they saw an astonishing sight. Sitting in a garden graced with slender bamboo and chrysanthemums was their mother, youngest brother, and an elegant woman who appeared to be his wife. These three were surrounded by laughing children and smiling neighbors. Everyone was enjoying the summer night, listening to the chirp! chirp! of crickets and sipping tea from light green cups.

And though the two brothers wanted to know how such a miracle had come to pass, they were too full of shame to knock on the gates of the great house. With their heads down they quietly departed—their lives empty—for long ago they had sold their souls for a single box of gold.

Like all great stories, this poetic tale can be interpreted in different ways; like a gem with many facets, it can be turned back and forth under the light of imagination and reflect back multiple meanings.

And, like many mythic tales, its characters can be viewed as elements of a single psyche. As such, this story communicates a great deal about the process of soul development. It teaches us that our souls are deepened when we confront Seas of Ice and Walls of Fire. And it warns us that if we trade in the inexhaustible wealth that comes from realizing our soul's dreams, we can easily end up as beggars, forever barred from entering the great mansion of peace and prosperity.

This story also tells us that if we wish to turn our dreams into reality, we must engage with the world. Our dreams do not become real if we remain sheltered within the safe little cottage of the known. We need to go out into the world, for it is in overcoming the trials that await us there that we become strong. More than anything, inner fortitude is what we need to transform our visions into reality. If we wish to live in a world that reflects our soul's deepest desires, we must be prepared to give our all—our blood and tears. And we must absolutely believe that we can achieve the impossible, that we can cross Seas of Ice and Walls of Fire without flinching.

The story also describes some of the negative voices you will hear as you seek to bring your dream into the world of space and time. Whether these voices belong to external or internal critics, their message will always be the same. Like the two elder brothers in the tale, these voices will try to convince you that you do not have the power or talent to change the way things are. They will try to persuade you that you are unreasonable for expecting more from life than just surviving or getting by.

Afraid of our magician's ability to extend the boundaries of the phenomenal world, these destructive voices declare, in solemn tones, that life's limits are more real than its possibilities. Often these destructive critics are obsessively concerned with issues of

security. Repeatedly they urge us to stop weaving our dream bro-
cades and go to market. Although issues of physical survival are very
real and need to be seriously addressed, we must never let these concerns take precedence over what must be done to accomplish our
soul's deep dreams *if we desire to live rich and fulfilling lives.*

Finally, this story provides us with information concerning what
needs to be done to bring the mind's pictures to life in the outer
world. It clearly teaches that if we are to realize our soul's dreams, we
cannot depend on logic and reason alone. We must permit ourselves
to be led by the deerskin shoes of instinct and let ourselves be carried along by the white horse of unconscious imagination.

The widow's older sons do not understand the role imagination
plays in accomplishing the seemingly impossible. The wise old
crone—an embodiment of the Higher Self—understands that if the
two elder brothers do not first have the power to *imaginatively picture* crossing the Wall of Fire and the Sea of Ice, they will not be
capable of accomplishing such feats in real life. Recognizing their
weakness, she dismisses them with gold.

Unlike his older siblings, Wang doesn't recoil when he learns of
the obstacles he must overcome before reaching the brocade. Without hesitation, he knocks out his two front teeth—an action that
symbolizes his willingness to fuse the rational mind with its analytical ability to tear apart, bite through, and separate, to the power of
the unconscious imagination.

To accomplish our dreams, we must marshal the powers of our
imagination; we must paint a vivid picture in our minds of what we
want, and then believe that we possess the power to bring those
images to life. Like the widow in the tale, it is crucial to imbue these
mental pictures with deep emotion—our blood and tears. And like

Wang, the tale's youngest son, we must venture out into the world and do the physical work necessary to bring our mental pictures to life.

Both prior to and during the writing of this book, I activated the helping power of my unconscious imagination by visualizing images of a completed book. To weave these inner images with a sure hand, I spent hours in bookstores exploring and analyzing books relating to my subject. I examined covers and titles and stood near the cash register, imagining that the people in line were purchasing the book I had written.

Before going to sleep at night, and first thing in the morning, I reviewed these images. And though the book was still in progress, I envisioned it as if it had already been written and published. I saw it and turned it over and over in my hands, delighting in its creamy white pages, running my fingers over its smooth cover, inhaling the fresh smell of ink and paper. I then let these consciously created images fall into the well of my unconscious and trusted that its wisdom would direct my actions and choices in such a way that my inner pictures would eventually take shape in outer reality.

Because they promised a positive outcome, these mental pictures gave me the staying power to sit at my "loom"—my computer—hour after hour. They helped me keep moving in the direction of my dream, even when I felt burned by rejection and frozen by creative despair—my Walls of Fire and Seas of Ice. Most importantly, visualizing the book in its finished form fired up my unconscious. In its mysterious way, it led me to people and situations that helped me make my dream come true.

Visualization requires that we create clear mental paintings that vividly detail our dream in its fully realized state. In these mental pictures we must imagine ourselves interacting with our dream imagery with positive and powerful emotion. For example, if I visualized someone reading my book, I did not simply see them reading; rather, I imagined myself thrilled by their interest.

Your visualizations need to be clear and vivid, but they do not have to describe all the details of what you seek. Leave some space for the unconscious imagination to work its magic. The unconscious imagination has a great deal more wisdom than the conscious mind, and so we do not want to inhibit or limit that power by being overly specific. This idea is expressed in the story about the dream brocade. The widow's brocade did not include the red-robed spirit from Sun Mountain. The spirit came into the widow's world as a result of the journey undertaken by the youngest son on the back of the white horse, emblem of the unconscious.

When we have done everything possible to realize our inner pictures, there exists a very great probability that these pictures will take shape in the world of space and time. And when the soul's needs have been honored, peace opens in the heart. Gifted with this peace, we can finally relax. Like the widow in the tale, we too can sit by crystal pools, and surrounded by friends and family, sip tea from light green cups, listen to the night crickets, and know a happiness too deep for words.

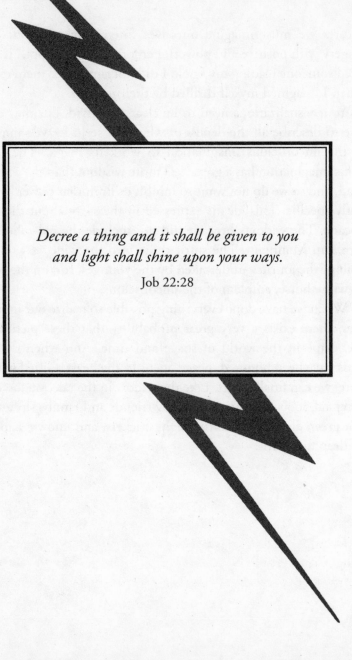

*Decree a thing and it shall be given to you
and light shall shine upon your ways.*

Job 22:28

CHAPTER SEVEN

THE TALISMAN
◆ AFFIRMATION ◆

When I was ten years old, I received my first violin. I loved its glossy wood, its block of amber resin for the bow, and the crushed velvet interior of its case. But far surpassing this visual beauty was the sound of the instrument, produced by the just right pressure of fingers and bow. With delight, my ear traveled through musical landscapes—high silver forests and deep rivers of sound.

Because I had a passionate desire to make the instrument sing, I did not look forward to recitals. Assailed by nervousness, I feared I could not create the strong, musical sound that so clearly sang out in my inner ear. Recognizing that something beyond dutiful practicing was required, I began preparing for concerts by repeating a little chant. Prior to each recital, I wrote down and repeated, silently and aloud, these words: "My fingers move well; my instrument sings."

These words became my talisman. I believed they would protect me from jittery nerves. Amazingly, they did just that. And if I had practiced sufficiently, the recitals usually went well.

In retrospect, I realize I had been using a results-oriented, thought conditioning technique called affirmation. Simply put, an affirmation is a consciously created declaration—whether written or spoken aloud or silently—that asserts the existence of a desired object or condition. Affirmations are powerful, dream-realizing tools. Like dream-supporting visualizations, positive affirmations program our subconscious mind to fulfill our goals or intentions. They also create feelings of expectancy and hope. In turn, these feelings lead us to and attract life's helping forces.

Additionally, affirmations can increase our sense of control, and as proven in countless studies in the field of personality research, people who believe that they can determine the course of their own lives have a much higher success rate than those who believe in only luck or fate.

During the period directly following my father's auto accident, I sat in the Intensive Care Unit, listening to Mary, the woman mentioned in Chapter Four, as she recited a fragment from the Twenty-Third Psalm: "The Lord is my Shepherd; I shall not want, He maketh me to lie down in green pastures; he leadeth me beside the still waters; He restoreth my soul. . . ."

Despite her terrible situation, Mary affirmed that she had no need, no want. She declared that the fortitude needed to cope with her painful trial was available to her. And though the heart-wrenching pain of a child's death would turn any parent's soul into a barren desert, Mary affirmed, through her recitation of the Twenty-Third Psalm, that green pastures and healing waters existed for her; she affirmed that her ravaged soul was restored. Mary's affirmation —in this case, a prayer—provided her with the strength she needed to suffer her ordeal with grace and dignity.

Unlike a wish, which admits to the possibility that a desired goal or condition may not happen, an affirmation powerfully asserts that what we desire to be, do, or have *already* exists. As established in the previous chapter, something believed to be true in one's innermost self very often takes form in outer reality. When we affirm something, our conscious mind communicates a direct message to our subconscious. Susceptible to suggestion, our subconscious will do everything possible to help us realize our heart's desire.

To effectively program our subconscious, it is necessary to practice our affirmations on a daily basis. Many dream-realizing techniques, such as affirmation, fail to give us the results we want, not because they lack in power, but because we use them *only* during times of difficulty, stress, and despair.

The following tale from Tibet illustrates how a repeated affirmation, when blended with correct outer action and contemplation, leads to the realization of a dream.

*I*n the time of the Buddha, there lived two brothers. The younger, whose name was Sonam, was simpleminded. Try as he might, he could not remember any of the holy scriptures his father tried to teach him; the verses escaped him, running through his mind like nectar through a sieve. The older brother was extremely intelligent; he was well-liked and admired by the Brahmins.

When the father of these two boys died, the elder brother entered a monastery. Sonam longed to join the order, but was barred from entering; the monks believed him too stupid for the rigors of spiritual study. Without his father's support, Sonam was reduced to a miserable existence. He moved to an impoverished neighborhood and spent his days begging for food and seeking shelter.

Feeling pity for the feeble-minded Sonam, the older brother sug-

gested that he request help from Ananda, the Buddha's assistant. With a reverent heart, Sonam approached Ananda, and sensing the young man's purity, Ananda performed his ordination and gave him a simple verse to memorize. The verse extolled the value of giving up negative action and thought, and praised the worth of healthy thinking, virtuous action, and selfless service.

For many weeks, Sonam tried to memorize the verse, but it was of no use—he could not retain a single line. In despair, he returned to Ananda.

"One greater than I must help you," Ananda said. With these words, he departed, leaving Sonam alone. Ashamed and confused, Sonam began to weep. It was like this that the Compassionate One first saw him.

The Buddha said, "You suffer this mental condition because of your past life. In that lifetime you were a Brahmin who stole the words of other scholars. You did not share your wealth, and often grew angry with others because of their inability to understand you. And you pretended to have spiritual knowledge you did not possess. Because of this, your intelligence is now limited. But do not worry, Sonam. Enlightenment can still be yours."

The Buddha took Sonam as his own pupil. He gave him a simple mantra to memorize. He told Sonam to repeat: "Remove the dust, scrape the mud." He then instructed Sonam to daily sweep the temple and scrape the mud from the monks' shoes. To ensure that Sonam would not lack for things to do, the Buddha ordered the mud to tenaciously cling to the monks' shoes and for the dust to be plentiful.

Though the other monks laughed at Sonam, he paid them no heed. As instructed by the Buddha, he diligently swept the dust from the tem-

ple floor and scraped the mud from the monks' shoes. As he did these simple tasks, he repeated, "Remove the dust, scrape the mud," and after several months, the mantra had engraved itself on his heart.

Because the words were so simple, Sonam was able to meditate on their meaning. Was the Compassionate One telling him to remove outer dust and mud or inner dust and mud? And if the dust and mud were the dust and mud on his soul, what were they?

One day, after many years of silently repeating and meditating, "Remove the dust, scrape the mud," a holy verse came to him—its precious words shining like candles in the darkness of his mind. He did not remember having heard this verse before, and even if he had, he never would have been able to retain or master its difficult language.

In long, ornate lines, the verse described how a wise person removes the mud and dust of attachment, anger, and delusion from his soul. The verse taught Sonam that if he could do this, he would be set free.

Suddenly, the broom fell from Sonam's hands, and like a thunderbolt he pierced the veil of illusion, and truth and understanding flashed in his soul. For a moment he stood still, and then, his heart overflowing, Sonam picked up the broom and resumed sweeping—his eyes delighting in the sight of the glittering, light clouds of dust now rising up from the old wooden floor.

This tale teaches us that the way to enlightenment is through spiritual practice, not excessive intellectual understanding. As the poet, John Keats, writes: "I am certain of nothing but the truth of imagination and the holiness of the heart's affections."

This story also shows how a mantra, which, like non-petitionary prayer, is a kind of affirmation, can help achieve a desired condition.

The mantra spoken by Sonam, when combined with right action and contemplation, enabled him to pierce the veil of illusion.

From this tale, we learn that we should keep our affirmations succinct and simple. Affirmations that are too wordy or focus on too many outcomes lose their power. This story also teaches us to keep our affirmations within the realm of our ability. Though an affirmation should not be unduly constricted by our current condition and experience, effective ones must express ideas that our conscious mind deems plausible.

For instance, if a sixty-year-old person affirmed that he or she is an Olympic gymnast, there would be little chance for such an affirmation to actualize in the outer world. Given the physical rigors and age limitations of this profession, the conscious mind would reject this idea. An affirmation can describe a condition that doesn't yet exist, but that condition must seem plausible to the conscious mind.

Despite the fact that as a monk, enlightenment was Sonam's ultimate goal, the Buddha instructs him to repeat, "Remove the dust, scrape the mud," rather than "I am enlightened, I pierce the veil of illusion." Given Sonam's development at the time he encountered the Buddha, his conscious mind would have regarded such a statement as untrue.

Also, affirmations that focus on what must be done to realize a dream, rather than on the dream itself, are far more potent. I tag these *prescriptive affirmations,* as they prescribe what actions must be taken to reach a desired goal or intention.

For example, if your dream is to have a happy relationship with your partner, possible affirmations might focus on the activities that could lead to this kind of relationship. Affirmations could include things such as: my partner and I treasure talking together . . . we sit peacefully over steaming coffee mugs . . . we lovingly support each other in our individual struggles . . . we are joyously playing with our children . . . we happily watch sunlight streaming through our windows.

Affirmations, like visualizations, must be written or silently spoken in a lively way, using action words, rich with emotional feeling and sensory imagery. Affirmations should not be written or spoken in a flat, robot-like manner that has no energy or charge. Such affirmations will fail to excite the part of our mind that puts magic into action. Although not stated directly in the above story, it is clear that Sonam's fierce love of and desire for enlightenment permeated his mantra.

When you create an affirmation, it is helpful to use words that trigger a positive emotional response. In the example on relationships cited earlier, words such as "treasure," "lovingly," and, "joyously," and colorful descriptions such as "steaming mugs of coffee," and "sunlight streaming through windows," evoke (for me) strong and positive feelings. As a magnifying glass increases the heat of the sun's rays, intense feelings and vivid, evocative language magnify the power of an affirmation.

However, it is important to bear in mind that *intense* feeling is different than *tense* feeling. Affirmations are most powerful when practiced in a relaxed mood. At these times the unconscious mind is most open to suggestion. Repetitive activities lull the mind into this receptive state. Secular variants of Sonam's temple sweeping and mud scraping could include washing the dishes, folding clothes, running or walking, riding the train, swimming, climbing a Stairmaster, drumming, chanting, or controlled breathing. Just don't let the repetitive nature of the activity dull the passion that you pour into your affirmation.

Furthermore, we should not use affirmations to suppress troubling emotions or make ourselves feel temporarily better. Not only is it important to acknowledge our real feelings and look into their deeper causes, but as previously mentioned, affirmations are rarely effective if they are used only during times of stress.

In the tale of *Aladdin and the Magic Lamp,* the magician utters a secret incantation over the stone that blocks the entrance to a cavern containing gold, jewels, and the wonderful old lamp. The magician's incantations cause the stone to roll aside, and the treasure hidden within becomes accessible. In another tale from the Arabian Nights, a character named Ali Baba recites a secret formula and his words, "Open sesame," also move a stone that blocks the entrance to a treasure-filled cave.

Our affirmations, like the mysterious words spoken in these and countless other ancient tales, are the "Open sesame" that can help remove the heavy boulders standing between us and our dreams. And when we actualize the dreams that embody our life purpose, we discover a world of riches. When we live our dreams, we see things differently. Our eyes, like the eyes of Sonam, are endowed with the power to see pure light and glittering clouds, whereas before they saw only dust.

I thank you God for this most amazing day:
for the leaping greenly spirits of trees
and a blue true dream of sky;
and for everything which is natural
which is infinite which is yes

e.e. cummings

CHAPTER EIGHT

THE ANTELOPE'S GIFT
• GRATITUDE •

Through my window is a magnificent panorama. In the distance are the Palisades—giant rock formations covered with trees whose leafy tops catch the light of the sun as it rolls in and out of fast moving clouds. In counterpoint to this fast-moving energy, is the river below, its silver waters slowly wending toward the sea. Inside, more images evoke feelings of gratitude. On the window sill stands a Buddha, his eternal belly laugh masterfully caught by a Filipino woodcarver. On a chest beneath the Buddha are several quartz crystals, flashing and winking in split seconds of sunlight. A little grouping of photos—family, friends, and far away places—rounds out the charm of this display.

Further contributing to the richness of all this is my feeling of contentment, arising from the fact that I am engaged in a cherished activity: sitting and writing in a clean and peaceful apartment, a cup of tea nearby, its steam swirling upward, sweetening the air. Taking all this in, I am overwhelmed with a soul-warming feeling that can best be described as gratitude.

When we express gratitude for the good in our lives, we focus on what we *have* rather than what we *lack*; this recognition promotes well-being. When we express gratitude, we perceive ourselves as recipients of blessings rather than as struggling victims of an uncharitable fate. If repeatedly experienced, this image of ourselves reaches deep into our subconscious, sending into action all the powers of the subconscious to transform our inner beliefs into outer realities.

It is also important to be grateful—within reason—for all that challenges, saddens, angers, or frustrates us. As many tales reveal, jewels are often guarded by serpents and toads, creatures associated with the repugnant. Similarly, painful experiences are not meaningless; as everyone knows, a pearl can be found within the roughest shell. In the act of cracking open pain's shell, we are strengthened. This strength helps us overcome the obstacles that stand between us and our dreams.

I once had a workshop participant whose story beautifully illustrates the power of gratitude. This woman, Marisol, bore the scars of inner-city life. Despite the fact that one parent was a hard and steady worker, the other was alcoholic and often absent. The abuse Marisol suffered at the hands of this parent, when combined with her childhood education in the dog-eat-dog, do-or-die mean streets of the city, eventually led to her downfall. Her soul collapsed, and she wound up in the hellish underworld of drugs.

When Marisol turned thirty, she became pregnant. She also learned she was HIV positive. Motivated by fear and impending motherhood, she suddenly had one dream—to change her life. Toward this end, she began seeking emotional, spiritual, and medical help. Because she expressed profound and genuine gratitude to the administrators, counselors, facilitators, peers, and medical practitioners who became involved in her case, many went out of their way to provide her with assistance. Their support, combined with her own formidable powers, created a miracle. As of this writing,

Marisol is well on her way to a recovery from substance abuse, and despite the HIV, her health is good. The energy she once freely burned in the bowl of a crack pipe is now being used to create a future, however long or short it may be, for herself and her daughter —a twinkle-eyed, chubby-legged toddler of two.

Feeling and expressing gratitude for the good we have in our lives does not mean we need to passively accept those aspects of our lives that are not working. However, while engaged in the process of creating more fulfilling lives, it is essential to focus on our wealth, not our poverty. Though we must fully acknowledge the troubled areas of our lives, and consciously make an effort *not* to avoid our problems, it is imperative that we simultaneously find things to praise. Complaining only focuses the mind's attention on lack, and what the mind focuses on gradually takes shape in the outer world.

It is not easy to live in a state of gratitude. The deep emotional and physical troubles that result when we live out of alignment with our purpose makes it difficult to see the embers shining in the blackened coals, but we must try.

One way to fan these embers into shining flames, is to train yourself to be more aware of the soul-nourishing beauty around you. Even seemingly small events such as quenching your thirst with a frosty glass of water, luxuriating beneath a quilt on a blustery morning, watching the breeze undo a dandelion puff, or listening to a chorus of crickets singing on a star-spangled, moon-gold night, are things that, if respectfully regarded, can evoke your gratitude. Keeping a list that records the wonders you daily encounter, or surrounding yourself with things that evoke feelings of gratitude, such as a picture of a parent, child, or friend, a sea polished pebble, or a letter, are ways that you can remind yourself of your wealth.

When we cultivate and express gratitude for our spiritual, emotional, and physical treasures, we radiate positive feelings. In turn, these positive feelings attract people to us and our enterprises. No one can realize a dream without the support of others; so the ability to radiate *sincere* good feeling plays a crucial role in our dream-realizing quest. Far from being naive, a deeply and sincerely cheerful attitude is like the sun; it causes things to grow.

Cultivating such an attitude does not ignore the dark side of our lives, whether that darkness is present within ourselves or others. A spiritually developed person will not credit the world for containing more good than it actually does. However, when we hold a deeply cheerful attitude, the world's darkness does not eclipse our own light and the abundant light that is present in the world.

The oral tradition is filled with tales that attest to the importance of expressing gratitude. The story below, which is well-known throughout Central Asia, is one of them. My retelling is based on a variant I first heard while traveling in Turkey. Searching for stories, I journeyed to little gypsy villages, high up in the mountains near the Black Sea. I stayed for several days in one of these villages with my traveling companion and translator. It was on a cold night, while huddled with a group of villagers before a roaring fire, that I first heard this story.

In a time that was and a time that was not, there lived a man named Mustapha. Mustapha was very poor; he had to beg for his food and sleep on the street's hard pavement.

One morning Mustapha was awakened by the sound of a distant bell. He arose from sleep and looked down the road. He saw a man coming towards him, leading a donkey-pulled cart. When the man got close, Mustapha saw that the cart was laden with a large cage containing three antelopes. The man said to Mustapha, "Would you like to buy an antelope?"

Mustapha was about to angrily retort, "I am a poor man. I have no money for antelopes!" But before he uttered these words, one of the animals stuck its nose between the bars of the cage and pleaded, "Buy me with the coins in your pocket. You will not be sorry."

Mustapha was so taken aback by the talking animal that he pulled out his few remaining coins and handed them to the man. The seller freed the antelope, and continued on his way, ringing his bell and crying, "Antelopes for sale! Antelopes for sale!"

Perplexed, Mustapha scratched his head and looked at the creature. "Now what am I going to do with you?" he said. The antelope was quick to respond. "Do not worry, I am your fortune." And with these words, the dreamy-eyed creature sprinted away.

The dispirited Mustapha sat down. Now he had no antelope and no coins to buy a bit of food. Well, serves me right, he angrily thought. Who but a fool purchases a talking antelope?

Now as Mustapha was sitting and trying to figure out how he would get some breakfast, the antelope was speeding through the streets, faster than the wind, faster than light. Soon the city was far behind. Where the animal went, no one knows, but when it returned, a heart-shaped ruby gleamed in its mouth. The animal knelt before Mustapha and dropped the jewel at the beggar's feet.

Mustapha rubbed his eyes in astonishment. Then, wasting no time, *he went to the bazaar and sold the ruby. With this money, he built a house, and next to the house he constructed a stall for the antelope. He sanded the floor and covered it with fresh yellow hay.*

Filled with gratitude, Mustapha spent hours in the stall, stroking the antelope's head. Thankful to Mustapha for giving it freedom, the animal continued to bring him precious stones—rubies, diamonds, and emeralds of all size and shape.

But as time passed, Mustapha started taking his good fortune for granted: he became more and more involved with his sherbets and danc-ing girls and soon forgot all about the antelope. Yet the gazelle was not completely ignored. Mustapha's new wife, Fatoush, loved the animal and continued to bring it food.

One day, when Fatoush approached the antelope, her heart sank. The poor beast was quivering; its eyes were cloudy, its nose rough and dry.

"What is wrong?" Fatoush asked. The antelope whispered, "I fear I shall die unless Mustapha brings me a bowl of honey and dates."

Fatoush went to her husband and repeated the antelope's request. But Mustapha dismissed her with a wave of his hand. "I have more important things to do than worry about the whims of an antelope," he said. "Feed it yourself!"

Fatoush returned to the ailing creature, carrying a bowl of dates and honey. She stroked its poor, fevered body, and explained that Mustapha would not be coming. "But do not worry, I have brought you food, and will continue to do so." The antelope replied, "Your kindness is much appreciated, but it will not save my life. Mustapha must bring me the food. Please ask him again."

Fatoush returned to Mustapha and begged him to respond to the gazelle's request. Once more, Mustapha refused. Heartsick, Fatoush

*returned to the antelope and said, "Mustapha is not coming, but please
. . . eat." The gazelle closed its eyes and whispered, "I cannot."*

*That night, Mustapha asked Fatoush how the animal was faring.
"The antelope is dead," she bitterly replied. "It longed for you to bring it
food, and you refused. And as for you, I am dead, too! I cannot live with
a man like you! Tomorrow morning, I return to my family's house!"*

"Who needs you, anyway?" Mustapha retorted.

*That night, Mustapha dreamt of the antelope. In his dream the
creature said, "Mustapha, I brought you rubies and diamonds and
emeralds. Why did you forget me?" Mustapha watched as the antelope's
body began to dissolve. It grew more and more transparent, and then it
vanished completely.*

*When Mustapha opened his eyes again, it was morning. To his sur-
prise and horror, he discovered that he was no longer a rich man lying
in a feathered bed. He was now, as before, a beggar stretched out on a
stony street. Mustapha sat up and pulled his ragged jacket about his
shivering body. But his efforts were in vain—his cloak's tattered cloth
offered little protection against the blowing wind.*

Traditionally, animals such as the antelope have been thought of
as a symbol for the soul, and so on one level this story is about the
importance of feeding our soul. It also teaches the importance of
gratitude.

In the beginning of the tale, Mustapha expresses his gratitude to
the antelope: he builds the animal a fine stall and in response, the
animal continues to bring him jewels. But as the story progresses,
Mustapha stops feeling and expressing his gratitude. As a result of
this, his good fortune slowly begins to fade—an idea symbolically

expressed by the antelope's gradual weakening. In the end, Mustapha is returned to his impoverished condition.

The tale illustrates the idea that ingratitude is one of the quickest ways to repel the blessings that come our way. Our lack of gratitude manifests itself in myriad ways. One of these ways is the careless manner with which we use the things of the world—the gifts of a generous earth and hardworking humanity.

In our rush to do what we feel needs doing, we seldom reflect on the gifts we receive. We drive through amazing landscapes—spectacular displays of color and shape—but hardly notice. We eat an animal or plant, without so much as a silent word of thanks to the living thing that gave its life for our nourishment. Others do kind or helpful things for us, and we minimize their efforts or do not express adequate appreciation for their service. Wrapped up in the demands of our personal lives, we too often ignore, or even speak harshly to the network of friends, family members, and colleagues who support us in our journey through life. The very source of existence, the sun, is all too often greeted with a curse; it is seen as a demanding intruder ordering us to throw off the covers of sleep and begin the activities of an unwanted day.

Many Native American traditions emphasize the importance of expressing gratitude, particularly to the earth. Like many, I am drawn to the solemn beauty of the Navajo Blessingway Chants. It is said that the power of these ceremonial songs is so great it can bring the afflicted individual back into harmony with his or her world.

Not long ago I saw a documentary in which a Navajo singer recited a version of the Beautyway Chant to quell the anxiety of an elderly woman. The singer described the patient's connection to the inner forms, the soul and spirit of the mountains, herbs, evergreens, morning mists, clouds, gathering waters, dew drops, and pollen. By helping this person feel kinship with the rich and wild beauty around her, the singer contributed to her healing.

In a similar way, the act of feeling and expressing gratitude is good and powerful medicine. When we feel connected to the richness surrounding us, we cannot help but feel blessed. And though life and suffering are intertwined—paired together as rainbows and storm clouds, sunlight and shadow, sickness and health—gratitude, like faith, helps us understand that suffering is not the whole picture.

When we focus our attention on the people—both known and unknown—who help us, the natural world that sustains and nourishes us, the things of beauty and acts of kindness that grace our lives, and most importantly, the Spirit that gives shape and motion to all things, we are able to escape the ego's small and stifling cage. When this happens, our souls, like the fleet-footed antelope in the tale, are free to enrich our lives with precious and radiant things. Feeling and expressing gratitude gives us a positive vision of ourselves and our world. Believing ourselves blessed, we attract blessings, including one of the greatest blessings of all: the chance to travel the path that leads to the fulfillment of our life's purpose.

*The whole idea of compassion
is based on a keen awareness of the
interdependence of all these living beings,
which are all part of one another and
all involved in one another.*

Thomas Merton

CHAPTER NINE

DIAMONDS AND ROSES
• COMPASSION •

*M*any years ago, my brother arrived home from school, his third grade face wet with tears. After some gentle prodding, my mother discovered that he was sad because a classmate had been taunted for wearing glasses. Although my brother did not wear glasses, nor could I remember him ever having been singled out by his peers for a personal trait deemed offensive, his fledgling soul experienced his classmate's pain as his own. His being was hurt by the cruelty meted out to another.

My young brother's ability to suffer with a fellow human being showed him to be well advanced on the spiritual path. In the early stages of soul development, our compassion for others is summoned by situations that trigger our own memories and experiences of pain. In a more developed soul, compassion is evoked because one has awakened to the fact that all life—in all its forms—is one and the same. When we are genuinely compassionate, our feelings derive not from how another's pain reminds us of our own, but from a much deeper source.

Rich, nurturing compassion flows from our ability to participate in the pain of others because we have had some fundamental, almost mystical recognition of life as one living, breathing organism. As Chief Seattle taught, life is a web, and each living thing is a strand of that web. A truly compassionate individual is able to see beyond the soul's container, its physical form. When someone recognizes and salutes the inner beauty of every human being, profound growth occurs, both for the beholder and the beheld.

Compassion dissolves the "I" that creates our illusion of separateness. Because compassion is rooted in a feeling of oneness, it is not selective. When any part of the whole is injured, each part suffers. The developed soul suffers as much for the perpetrator as for the victim; both are a part of the same living body, and both are trapped in the chains of suffering, albeit suffering of a different order.

This idea became clear to me several years ago while giving storytelling workshops in the deep South. An African-American participant, whom I will call Marva, told a story about an ugly racial incident that happened to her during the early years of school integration. When she entered a previously all-white school, a boy greeted her with cruel racial slurs . . . "Nappy head . . . nappy head . . . you are nothing but a nappy-headed nigger and we don't want you in this school!" With moving words, Marva described how proud she had been of her hair and how badly the boy's words hurt her. She described how she had run home to her mother, crying bitterly.

A good many of the other workshop participants—African-American and European-American, Asian-American, and Jewish-American—were deeply moved by Marva's story, some to tears, others to silence. However, one participant, also African-American and about the same age as Marva, remarked that as the story unfolded, she found herself experiencing sorrow for the taunting boy as well as for Marva. "That boy is trapped in his social conditioning," she quietly said. "He speaks from fear. He will live and die with fear in his heart, and this is a terrible thing."

This woman's compassion stood in shining contrast to the responses of some of the other participants who either remained unmoved, made harsh references toward white people, or unconsciously held up Marva's story as a dark mirror reflecting memories of their own societal rejection.

Unfortunately, one of the unforeseen by-products of the multicultural movement in American society has been the vilification of all things white, European, and male, and the deification of the victim, either by the victims themselves, or by individuals who support their cause.

Such a response is understandable, given the years of oppression of non-whites in American culture, particularly African-Americans and Native Americans. Nonetheless, breaking the world into white and non-white, male and female, or even oppressor and victim, serves no purpose except to perpetuate the illusion of separateness. Such an attitude is not conducive to spiritual release. Life is one, and all attempts to support or prolong the illusion of separateness lead to suffering. As India's sacred scripture, the Bhagavad Gita, teaches: "Separateness is a mirage. The world is whole."

This idea does not imply that individuals or groups who cause injury to other living creatures—whether that injury is physical, spiritual, or psychological—should be tolerated. Nor does the idea that all life is one suggest that people who have been physically abused or psychologically diminished silently accept their persecution. But as we condemn those who perpetrate acts of cruelty, we must simultaneously bear in mind that those perpetrators are not separate beings. They are a part of us, just as we are a part of them, as difficult as this is to admit. If we don't think this way, we only continue the illusion of separation.

The greatest challenge we face is to see each individual as part of one gigantic living, breathing organism. A compassionate person understands that a part of the organism may be ill and in desperate need of healing. Such an understanding, as pointed out by the Buddha and other liberation teachers, will eventually set humanity free from the binding chains of the fundamental source of the world's misery: the egotistical self.

Recently, I heard a moving story that attests to the power of compassion. Years ago, I had a friend who was a student teacher in a rough city housing project in San Francisco. One day, a five-year-old came running to him, tears streaming down his cheeks, blood pouring from his nose and lip. Sobbing, the boy explained that a girl named Naomi, a twelve-year-old, had punched him in the face. Within moments, Naomi came up and yelled that the younger boy got what he deserved. "He was bothering me!" she cried. As my friend related, he was just about to give Naomi a tongue-lashing, when his supervisor—a very wise older woman—stepped in. "You take care of the blood," the supervisor said to my friend. "I'll take care of the broken heart." The supervisor then took Naomi in her arms, and holding her close to her breast, she comforted the angry girl. "For the first time in three years, I saw Naomi weep," my friend recounted. He then concluded by saying that after this episode, the level of violence on the playground dramatically decreased.

Sincere compassion, like gratitude, opens the way to harmony within ourselves and harmony between ourselves and the world. And just as water and sunlight contribute to the growth of a plant, so harmony contributes to the realization of our dreams. Feeling at odds with the world—a condition that results when we look upon others as potential threats—produces feelings of hostility, suspicion, and resentment. These three emotions, more than any others, drain our energy—an energy that could be better applied to the tasks we must complete to realize our life's purpose.

So too, a lack of compassion inhibits the exchange of good will between people. True kindness and courtesy flow from one who perceives the holistic nature of the world. Kindness and courtesy enable us to get along with each other, and the ability to successfully interact with others is vital to realizing a dream. Our personal dreams are not reached without the support of countless hands, both seen and unseen.

Although often explained as simple narratives in which good is rewarded and evil punished, many of the world's folk and fairy tales provide examples of how the practice of compassion results in riches, both physical and spiritual.

As a child I loved the tale *Toads and Diamonds*. Like all mythic literature, it contains many possible meanings, but at its core it is a story about the value of compassionate action in the world.

A widow had two daughters. The older one, like her mother, was mean-spirited. The younger was gracious and sweet; kindness reigned, queen of her heart. The mother worshipped the older daughter and scorned the younger one. This girl had to do all the chores and was forced to walk miles each day to fill the family's water pitcher.

One day, while at the village fountain, an old woman, dressed in a patched and dirty robe, begged for a drink. The girl dipped her silver pitcher into the fountain's clearest part, drew some water, and helped the old woman drink. When the woman had finished, the young girl smiled and asked her if she needed anything else.

"No," she answered, "but I have a gift for you. Each time you speak, flowers and jewels shall drop from your mouth."

When the girl arrived home, her mother demanded an explanation for her tardiness. The girl begged forgiveness, and as she did so, two roses, several pearls and emeralds, and half a dozen diamonds tumbled from her lips.

"What's this? How has this miracle come about?" the mother gasped. The girl told her the story of the beggar woman at the well. As she spoke, more flowers and jewels cascaded from her mouth.

With hungry hands, the mother scooped up the treasures and then summoned her older daughter. She repeated the story of the old woman at the well, and concluded by saying, "Go to the fountain, and when an old woman appears and requests a drink of water, be sure to give her one."

"I don't think it's right for someone as fine as myself to go and gather water, much less serve it to anyone else!" the elder sister protested.

"Just go!" the mother shouted as she thrust the silver pitcher into the girl's unwilling hands. The eldest sister departed, leaving behind a trail of curses and complaints.

When she got to the fountain, an elegant lady dressed in flowing silks and velvet asked for a drink. "And why should I give you a drink?" the girl haughtily replied. "Do you think I am your servant?"

Now as it so happened, this woman was the same one who earlier had appeared in the guise of a beggar. Infuriated by the girl's rudeness, she said, "Every time you speak, toads and snakes will fall from your lips!" Terrified, the girl rushed home.

When the mother saw her daughter's frightened face, she cried, "What has happened to you?" The girl told her story, and as she spoke, snakes slithered from between her lips, and a pair of fat brown toads leapt forth.

"This is the fault of your sister!" the mother shrieked, as she looked aghast at the slippery creatures, now hopping and crawling across the floor. Hearing this and fearing a flogging, the younger girl fled into the forest. She hid among the sheltering trees, trembling and crying, not knowing what to do, her heart pounding with fear.

Just before nightfall, the girl heard a rustling in the distance. She looked towards the sound and saw an extraordinary sight. Coming through the trees, she saw a man on a fine steed, his face shining like the sun itself.

"What are you doing alone in the forest? Why are you weeping?" he asked. The girl told him of her predicament, and as she spoke, two roses, three milky white pearls, and a dozen sparkling diamonds dropped from her mouth.

Though astonished by the flowers and jewels, the regal youth, who was in fact the king's son, was more surprised and moved by the kindness that so clearly shone in her eyes. And in that moment, he fell in love with her and requested her hand in marriage. The girl accepted, overjoyed by fate's strange and miraculous twist.

As time passed, the elder sister became more and more hateful. Before long, even her mother wearied of her foul moods and ill temper. So she turned her out of the house and told her never to return. Unable to find anyone willing to take her in, the older daughter wandered alone, walking from village to village, growing weaker and weaker. One cold and snowy winter day, the exhausted girl, unable to take another step, dropped to the ground. She cried out for help, but no one came.

Helpless, she watched as the sun sank behind the hills, plunging the world into darkness. The girl lay in the snow for a long time, her frost-bitten toes and fingers aching and burning from the cold. She strained her ears, listening for the sound of another human being, even an ani-mal to comfort her, but the only thing she heard was the ice-loaded tree boughs, groaning and creaking in the wind.

This is more than a simple cautionary tale providing moral counsel on how the wicked are punished and the good rewarded. This story shows us that great gifts can be ours when we listen to the wisdom of the unconscious mind, symbolized by the image of the young girl filling her silver pitcher with water from the clearest part of the fountain and giving it to the old woman, symbol of our divine nature or Higher Self. When we quench the thirst of this part of our being, we receive great gifts. The tale also paints, in simple strokes, a picture of compassion or impersonal love in action.

By assisting the old woman, the young girl is embodying what the Buddhists call *karuna* or compassion: the loving feeling for others which is imbued with a desire to alleviate their suffering, regardless of their appearance. Her compassion transforms the younger daughter from a simple peasant to a queen—an outer condition reflecting the divine nature of her inner being. Whenever she speaks, she leaves a trail of beauty for others to follow.

Recently, I gave a series of storytelling and music concerts for groups of children with severe disabilities. Some of the children were terribly disfigured. I must confess that at first I had difficulty with my own feelings about this group. Yet when I was able to get beyond their physical forms and travel into their essential natures on waves of story and song, jewels and flowers really did appear—jewels in the shape of joy-lit eyes, and flowers in the form of twisted hands moving vine-like to the music.

Unlike the younger daughter in the tale, the older daughter is unable to create jewels and roses. Compelled by a need to separate herself from the world, she haughtily refuses the elegantly dressed woman's request for water. Controlled by an unhealthy ego that acts without the counsel of the soul, she is cut off from the human family. Her speech, the primary means of human communication, results in the production of toads and snakes, which even she finds repugnant. Her inability to empathize with others or see her role within the web of life, ultimately leads to her own lonely death.

The fact that the fairy in the story appears as both a beggar and an elegantly dressed woman of high social standing further indicates that this tale is one about compassion. Compassion must be given freely to all, not just to those obviously in need, such as the poor, the weak, the sick. Compassion is not selective; as already noted, it is an even, loving concern for all living things.

Although the connection between compassion and the realization of those dreams that express our life's purpose may seem strained or even contrived, the practice of compassion is actually one of the most powerful dream-realizing tools available to us provided that it is genuine compassion, and not doing good in the hope of receiving some kind of reward.

Our compassion frees us to see the larger truth that exists beyond our own prejudices, judgments, worries, and selfish concerns. Freed from the vanities that ultimately contribute only to suffering, pain, or the fleeting illusion of control, we become healthier as people. Compassion opens a window, not only to a greater patience with the shortcomings of others, but to our own as well. And when we are more forgiving, we are almost always gifted with greater psychic, psychological, and physical energy. In turn, this energy can help carry us further and further along the road leading to the full realization of our fondest dreams.

In dream, in night's vision,
God opens the ears of sleepers and
seals in instructions.

Job

CHAPTER TEN

NIGHTFISHING
• DREAMS •

*M*y metaphor-making mind has always loved the sight of fishing boats, decked out in a festival of fairylights, bobbing up and down on the sea's dark waters. I cannot help but liken these bright fishing boats to our night visions. Just as these boats shed light on the dark waters, and with their wide nets pull nourishment up from the sea, our night dreams shed light on the unknown areas of our lives, and with their wide nets fish up treasures from our deep mind.

Like the opening tale of this book, many mythic stories make reference to the power of dreams. In countless tales, a goal is reached or a life improved when a character heeds the instructions or inspirations provided in a dream. Although dreams can be triggered by many things—from the mundane to the magical—an important role they play in the human drama is to bring unconscious wisdom to the surface. Like the ancient oracles that advised the kings and queens in legends of times long past, dreams can answer the questions posed by the conscious mind. "Learn from your dreams what you lack," writes the poet W. H. Auden.

From the earliest times, dreams have been viewed as significant events. The Old Testament is a treasure trove of prophetic dreams and other visionary experiences—the dreams of Solomon, Joseph, and Jacob come readily to mind, as do passages of angelic instruction and descriptions of waking visions. The Koran tells us that Mohammed encouraged dream sharing among his disciples, and the Ancient Assyrians and Egyptians kept dream books that attempted to decode dream symbolism. The literature of Ancient Greece and India describes special shrines where, with the aid of herbal potions, visitors induced sleep and dreams. The dreams that occurred in these sacred incubators were considered of great importance. In ancient Japan, it was part of the emperor's sacred duty to retire to the Hall of Dreams to lay upon his *kamudoko,* or bed of polished stone. Here, he received dreams that enabled him to rule wisely and well.

In traditional Chinese belief, dreams were regarded as journeys taken by the soul, which during sleep, separated itself from the body. Freed from the physical world, the soul was able to communicate with ghosts and ancestors, gods and goddesses.

The importance of dreams in Native American cultures is particularly vivid. A Lakota story tells of how the ceremonial drum used in the powwow was given to the people through the vision of a young woman hiding in a lake, beneath a large lily pad. And in many traditional Indian cultures such as the Yaqui and Huron, the curers or medicine men used dreams to help them diagnose and treat illness.

Perhaps more than any other tribal group, the Senoi of Malaysia show a great respect for the power and importance of dreams. Each morning Senoi children share their dreams with tribal elders. As the elders listen, they praise any brave deeds the children may have performed in their dreams, and suggest ways that they might conduct themselves in future dreams. The elders also encourage the children to transform their dreams into songs and dances, masks, and other objects.

Dreams can be interpreted either on literal or symbolic levels, or on both levels simultaneously. For instance, if a person dreams that he or she has lost control of a car while driving, the dream may be communicating a literal message that the dreamer should drive with more care. Read on a symbolic level, this dream could be intimating that an important aspect of the dreamer's life has careened out of control and needs attention.

It is generally agreed that when dreams are meant to function as physical warnings, they use realistic or familiar imagery. But when dreams seek to communicate spiritual wisdom, they often speak in a numinous, other-worldly imagery. The dream of the turtle tattoo— the dream that revealed the theme of this book—falls into this latter category.

I recall another "big dream," a dream I had many years ago that, like the dream of the turtle tattoo, also answered a difficult question. I include it here to illustrate how to read a dream's symbolic language.

In this dream, I saw a green parrot, a black box, and flowing bands of waving colors. The parrot was floating up from the black box, riding on the colors. The colors were very strong; they appeared almost metallic, similar to the shiny rainbows that glide across the surface of oily puddles. Like the green parrot, these bright colors stood out in sharp contrast to the dream's black background. The dream ended with a shower of gold coins pouring from the heavens.

This dream occurred in my mid-twenties. At that time, due to economic concerns, I was in conflict about whether to continue working in theater or switch to a more lucrative field, like the law. The dream of the green parrot answered this question.

The parrot, like all birds, is a messenger of the spiritual world. Symbolically, it often represents the soul and is tied to the faculty of speech. Hence, the image of the green parrot pointed out the connection between my work in drama and my soul. The rainbow pouring forth from the box, especially in connection to the shower of gold coins, is symbolically connected to hope, aspiration, and deep-rooted desire. The darkness surrounding these boldly colored and brilliant things represented my confusion and my inability to see which way to go. This darkness intensified the colors: the green parrot, the rainbows, and the shower of celestial gold.

Given these symbols and their relationship to each other, the dream seemed to suggest that regardless of my economic concerns, I should continue to follow the path of art—the path of beautymaking and soulmaking. The shower of celestial gold at the dream's conclusion seemed to indicate that such work would eventually be rewarded.

Vast numbers of ancient tales underscore the idea that dreams are invaluable tools that assist us in realizing our goals and aspirations. The oral tradition abounds with tales that teach of the dire consequences that befall the one who fails to heed the information offered in a dream. Still others demonstrate how dreams can lead to the discovery of treasure or to the creation of items of value and beauty.

The following tale from Haiti is a typical example of a story that warns us of the perils that befall those who ignore the messages given in their dreams.

*T*wo *friends—one short and the other tall—were traveling together across the countryside. They were both poor and had left their village some months before, seeking a place where they might be able to improve their lot in life. One day, after hours of trekking, the taller of the two men sat down, saying he needed to rest. He urged his partner to continue, explaining that he would eventually catch up. And so the other man kept walking.*

When night came, he arrived at an orange tree. As his traveling partner had not yet caught up, he decided to stop and sleep. And so he stretched out beneath the tree's moonlit leaves and closed his eyes.

Before long, he began to dream. In his dream, a voice said, "The princess in the next village is very sick. Take a leaf from this orange tree and make it into tea. Give this tea to the princess, and she will be cured."

The man woke up, and following the instructions in his dream, he removed a leaf from the orange tree. He then put this leaf into his pocket and continued on his way.

When he reached the next village, he was surprised to see a sign posted on the gate of the king's house. The sign announced that his daughter was gravely ill and that a reward was being offered to the one who could cure her.

The man saw his opportunity. Boldly, he stepped up to the palace gates and explained his mission to the guard. He was let in and taken to the king. "I have come to cure the princess of whatever it is that ails her," he announced.

The king was skeptical. All the doctors in Haiti had failed. What could this tattered fellow do that these wise and learned men could not? Nonetheless, having nothing to lose, the king decided to give the ragged traveler a chance.

Following the instructions in his dream, the man tore the orange leaf into many small pieces. He brewed these pieces into a sweet-smelling tea and for several days spoon-fed this brew to the princess. With each passing day, the girl grew stronger and stronger, and after several days she was wholly cured. The king was overjoyed. The tattered man, too, was delighted. He married the princess and received a good portion of the king's estate as well.

Shortly after his marriage, he returned to the place where his traveling companion had paused to rest, many months before. After searching a bit, he found his friend living in a nearby village. The friend was still struggling to make ends meet. The man who had married the princess told him everything that had happened since they parted. He then gave the poor man a sack of gold and wished him well.

Once alone, the man thought, "If dreams helped him become rich, they can help me, too." When the moon was full, he went to the place where the orange tree stood. He stretched out beneath the rustling leaves and soon fell asleep.

As he slept, he dreamt. In his dream, a voice cried, "Get up! Go from this place! Wake up! Run!" But the dreamer was not satisfied—he wanted to hear about riches. And so he lay there, waiting for other messages.

In the morning, the people found a skeleton lying beneath the orange tree. The man who had ignored his dream had been devoured, his bones picked clean by wild dogs, wolf-monsters, and the evil night spirits.

This tale teaches us that not only must we heed our dreams, but we must realize that each person's path—even to a similar goal—is unique. We can learn from those who have gone before us, but we must not turn a deaf ear to our own unique voices that often come to us in sleeping dreams and waking visions. Slavishly following the way of others and refusing our own inner prompting may even result in physical death, as is the case in this Haitian tale.

This story reminds me of an amusing anecdote I recently heard. A man is caught in a flood. He tells himself not to worry for God will save him. Soon a helicopter flies overhead. The pilot drops a rope to the drowning man, but he refuses, confident that God will rescue him. Following the helicopter, a boat arrives. Though the flood waters reach his neck, the man again refuses the help. Just as the waters are about to cover him, a raft floats by. Again, confident that God will save him, the man allows the raft to drift by.

The waters rise higher and higher, and finally the man drowns. When he gets to Heaven and encounters God, he cries, "Why didn't you save me!" And God replies, "What are you talking about? I tried three times! I sent a helicopter, a boat, and a raft!"

This anecdote teaches, like the Haitian tale, that our conscious notions of how things ought to be can too often prevent us from either receiving the help we need or recognizing it when it comes. In dreams, visions, and flashes of intuitive insight, our unconscious is speaking. If we disregard its message, wishing things were different, we put ourselves in peril of being swallowed by wolf-monsters, demons, and wild dogs!

Unfortunately, the messages that come to us in dreams are not always as clear as those communicated in the Haitian tale. As a result, we must do some excavation if we wish to uncover the wisdom in our night visions. Although an in-depth exploration of decoding dreams falls outside the scope of this book, I would like to briefly describe two Jungian dream-decoding techniques that you can use to garner insights from your dreams. They are Amplification and Active Imagination.

Amplification requires that we break each individual dream image into its parts. For example, with the dream of the parrot, I free-associated on the words *green* and *bird* as well as on the image of the parrot itself. After delving into the various parts of each image, I related each individual image to all the other images presented in my dream.

The technique of Active Imagination instructs us to become more physically involved with the dream material. If you use this technique, you might take crayons, paints, or colored felt pens and draw pictures representing the objects in your dreams, allowing yourself to free-associate on the images as you draw. Curiously, when I drew the parrot in my dream, I also spontaneously drew a large-planked bridge leading to a wedding altar, although neither a bridge nor an altar appeared in my dream. This image suggested to me that the arts might also lead me to some sort of deep relationship—either sacred or profane.

To role-play a dream, you might pretend you are, in turn, the animals, people, or even objects in your dream. Act out what these things might say, think, or do. Or create a dialogue between the different animals, people, and objects in your dream.

The following are some basic rules to follow to get the most from your dreams:

- Keep a dream journal; immediately record your dreams; unless written down, most dreams quickly vanish.

- Pay particular attention to repeated dreams—they usually indicate a deep internal conflict.

- Imagine that every character or object in the dream represents an aspect of yourself; explore the thoughts and feelings you associate with each dream character, image, or object.

- Consult dream and symbol dictionaries and write down as many meanings for specific images as possible; after gathering universal (or archetypal) and culturally specific interpretations of your dream images, determine which of these universal or cultural associations feels right to you.

- Trace the common thread running through your dream imagery (i.e., in the parrot dream cited above, the brilliant green of the parrot, the rainbow, and the shiny gold coins all stood in stark relief to the dark background).

- Make a dream wheel: put a central image or part of an image from your dream at the wheel's hub, and at the end of each spoke radiating from this "hub," write down all the words and thoughts evoked by the image at your wheel's center.

Had I chosen to disregard the dream of the turtle tattoo, it is possible I would have never written this book. If this had been the case, I would have lost the spiritual, psychological, and physical treasure that poured into my life as a result of its creation. Just as one would not throw back a beautiful treasure fished up from the sea, one should not throw back the insights fished up from our unconscious waters. These insights, communicated in the strange and wonderful language of sleeping dreams and waking visions, are meant to be heeded.

The instructions our dreams communicate can help us make the sweet orange tea that cures those ailing parts of ourselves. They can help us transform the tattered aspects of our beings into royalty. When this happens, we, like the successful man in the story, can bring prosperity to ourselves and our communities.

All journeys have secret destinations
of which the traveler is unaware.

Martin Buber

CHAPTER ELEVEN

SECRET DESTINATIONS
◆ LETTING GO ◆

T here comes a time during our dream-realizing journey when we must, like skydivers, jump with full confidence into miles of blue nothingness. Provided that we have done everything possible to prepare for this leap, it is likely that our parachutes will open and carry us safely to our desired destination, or to another, better place.

Letting go in this way is different from giving up. Giving up issues from frustration, despair, or anger. Letting go comes from a place of peace, of knowing that you have done everything possible to realize your dream. When we surrender, we do not stop taking the actions required to realize our dream, but we do toss away the map of expectations. Surrendering requires that we mentally release ourselves from the thing we have been so persistently seeking.

I have always loved to imagine acts requiring that I let go of my knowable, safe, and controllable world and enter into mysterious realms. In my mind's theater, I often envision myself walking through trackless deserts, diving into roiling seas, or jumping from airplanes—parachuting down through miles of empty blue sky.

When we surrender, we stop struggling, striving, longing, wanting. Our egos hand over the compass to a far greater navigating

Power. It is often at this moment that the very thing we have been passionately seeking—or something much greater—miraculously appears, seemingly "out of the blue."

There is a Persian tale about a man and a pearl-guarding dragon. For most of his life, the man, in an effort to obtain the pearl, wages war against the dragon. At last, believing he has done everything possible to overcome the dragon, the man lays down his sword. At that moment, the dragon vanishes, and the man is free to lift the shining pearl from its nest.

My experience as a performing artist has taught me much about the benefits that come when one lets go. From years of experience, I know that it is only when I am able to fully surrender my conscious grasp on the story and its telling, that real stage magic happens.

Theatrical storytelling is a strange art. Few people are aware of the extensive work that goes into preparing a story to be performed. Perhaps the technical demands of this art form are obscured by the fact that we are all storytellers in a way that we are not all ballet dancers, opera singers, or instrumentalists. Whether the storyteller be a young child weaving a jumbled narrative about the day's events or an adult spinning overlapping experiences of despair and hope in a therapist's office, we human beings are story-making animals.

And yet, like all performing arts, developing a story for theatrical presentation—especially a mythic story from a culture different than one's own—is not a simple task. Variations of the tale must be examined, and the tale's cultural background carefully researched. The story's symbols must be decoded, and language, image, and plot choices made. Most importantly, the story has to be excavated for personal meaning. Without this intimate connection between the teller and the story, the story will remain, at best, a museum piece—a thing behind glass, interesting to look at, but bereft of transformational power.

After I have developed the story, I begin working with my musical partner, for I have always felt that music greatly contributes to the emotional power of a spoken story. Using world flutes, harps, and percussion, Paula creates a group of melodies and rhythms that we then mix into the story, modifying both the story and the music as we go along.

But even when the story and music seem blended to my satisfaction and appear ready to perform, it takes many public tellings before I can truly release my grip on the tale and let it take on a life of its own. For a long time, questions run through my mind, even as I perform: Is the story too long or too short? Is the pacing too slow or too fast? Are the music and words properly mirroring each other? Is the audience understanding the story's intended meaning, and if not, what can I do to make it clearer? And so forth and so on. As long as I am engaged in this analytical process, no transformative experience can happen. It is only when I release my conscious grasp on the story—when I let go of my concerns—that the story yields up its treasure.

Many mythic stories speak of the riches a person garners at the moment of surrender. The story below is one of them.

There once was a man who heard that an eagle feather symbolized the highest wisdom. Wanting this feather, the man thought of nothing else. When his children came to him, wishing to share their joy in a newly

found pebble or baby bird, he barely noticed. When they cried and needed his comfort, he ignored them. He did not taste the delicious foods his wife prepared, nor admire the baskets she wove. Day and night he thought only of the eagle feather.

One day, after many years had passed, the man realized that maybe he was not meant to receive such a feather. He understood that his obsession with the feather had blinded him to life. His children were now grown, and his neglected wife had become aloof and distant. Failing to share in his community, the man had no friends. Frightened and alone, he began praying, hoping the Creator would provide him with the medicine he needed to heal his sad and troubled heart.

When the man finished praying, he felt very peaceful. He began to walk home and noticed for the first time the setting sun, floating like a red swan in a lake of sky. He delighted in the snap and crack of twigs underfoot and the fragrance of wood smoke curling up from distant campfires. The sight of a boy skipping pebbles across a golden pond brought a smile to his face. Then, an amazing thing happened.

A shadow swept across the ground. The man looked up and saw an eagle high up in the sky. The eagle hovered overhead for a moment and then vanished into a glowing bank of clouds.

The man rubbed his eyes, wondering if the eagle had been real or only imagined. And then he saw it—a black and white feather floating to earth, zigzagging on the wind. The feather landed at his feet, and the man stooped to pick it up, recognizing it as the symbol of the highest wisdom, the eagle feather he had spent so many years seeking.

For a long time he gazed at the feather, turning it back and forth, touching its glossy surface, running his finger down its curved spine. Then he dropped the feather on the ground and continued on his way. If he hurried, he could make it home before dark.

One of the things this story teaches is that life can indeed be empty without our full and authentic participation in the lives of those around us. It warns us that we must always guard against the natural tendency to cut ourselves off from the human world when we are absorbed in the process of trying to translate a dream into reality. If we are to free ourselves from that which binds us, we must fully participate in the joys and sorrows of the human drama in all its messy splendor.

This story also teaches that it is when we let go of our desire that we receive the thing we seek. Of course, paradoxically, we cannot give something up that we haven't first desired. If the man in this tale had not longed for the feather, he would not have undertaken the journey required to find it, the journey that ultimately led him to wisdom, the "secret destination" he was really seeking all the while.

When we toss away the map of expectations and surrender to forces greater than our own, we increase our chance of reaching this secret destination. And while we may not have known it at the start of our journey, this secret destination was the impetus for our dream-realizing voyage all along.

In truth, everything we desire is a small part of some greater, unseen whole, just as the feather is part of the eagle. Seeking to fulfill a specific dream motivates us to walk the road leading to this whole. In this way, desire inspires and compels us to do what we need to do to reach our true destination—the secret destination of every quest. And though this secret destination may *include* the successful completion of our original aim, it always includes far, far more.

Two years ago, in early autumn, I began writing this book. Now, as it draws to a close, it is spring—the season of emergence, new beginnings, renewal. On the streets of New York City, flower vendors arrange their colorful displays, and people walk with bouncy steps. The shop windows gleam with sunlight's polish, and the dogs in Central Park leap and twirl, catching balls and Frisbees between their teeth. Pink buds are tucked into leafy cups, and a butterfly, fresh to the world, fans its wings dry.

The act of writing this book has taken me to an unforeseen destination. I have fulfilled one of my dreams, that of writing this book and finding a publisher for it. Yet I now understand that, while the successful completion of this project will bring a measure of happiness to me and ideally to others, the way to unconditional freedom involves much, much more than the completion of a single dream, no matter how powerfully or perfectly that dream expresses our purpose.

Already, life is challenging me with new difficulties, new obstacles to overcome. I now understand, in a way that I did not at the outset of this book, that the completion of one dream will not usher in a trouble-free existence, although certainly the successful completion of this dream—this book—will bring much needed improvement to my life. More importantly, through the process of creating this book, I have gained undreamed of strength that I can now use to overcome the challenges that, as this project draws to a close, are making themselves loudly heard.

This strength will also assist me in completing my next dream, as yet unknown, but one that I now understand will be only another stone on the many-stoned path leading to wholeness. I now see that the reason we have so many dreams to fulfill is because, as W. B. Yeats said so beautifully: "To seek God too soon is not less sinful than to seek God too late; we must love, man, woman or child, we must exhaust ambition, intellect, desire, dedicating all things as they pass, or we come to God with empty hands." It is through the process of realizing all the dreams that reflect our purpose that we slowly empty ourselves of ambition, intellect, and desire. This insight is one of the treasures that the turtle tattoo helped me to find.

Writing this book gave me another unexpected jewel. Because of the isolation required to reach this goal, I experienced, first-hand, how unsatisfying life can become if, in the process of fulfilling our individual destiny, we isolate ourselves from others. This insight was dramatically underscored by an experience I had as the writing of this book was drawing to a close.

A friend of mine, I will call her Nadine, is dying of cancer. Trying to spare her relatives the burden of planning and organizing her funeral, Nadine decided that, while she was still able, she would assist her family with the details of this painful task. Wanting a few non-family members present at the meetings she was organizing to address this issue, Nadine called and requested my presence.

In the past, had I received such a request, I would have felt torn —wanting to help, but at the same time, not wanting to lose precious writing time. I would be dishonest if I claimed to be entirely free of such feelings when I received Nadine's call, and yet I also recognized that these feelings were much less strong than they would have been in the past.

While I still believe that writing this book was a task of supreme importance to the development of my soul, I now understand that this dream, and all the other personal dreams I will seek to fulfill throughout my life, can never outweigh in importance the needs of another human being, such as my friend's request that I participate in her death.

I will never forget the afternoon I spent at Nadine's. With her mother, sisters, and their children, I sat in a simply furnished room, a little glass bowl of candy on the table—the silver wrappers glittering in the sun. A spring breeze floated through the open windows, transforming the sheer white curtains into things both ethereal and delicate, eternally beautiful.

Nadine's mother sat across from the billowing curtains. Throughout the meeting, she cooled herself with a large black fan, furiously waving it back and forth as if this motion could stem the tide of tears streaming down her cheeks, or its fast fluttering could push away Nadine's illness and impending death. Words such as mausoleum, service, priest, burial, cremation, and casket drifted through the air, wafting on currents of sadness and occasional humor, like so many ashes in the wind. All the while, Nadine's nieces and nephews drifted in and out of the room, expressing the common needs and complaints of childhood: more juice, food, an adult coloring companion, a tormenting sibling to be silenced. And more often than not, it was Nadine who got up and tended to their needs.

Each time Nadine excused herself to respond to the children's needs, I found myself reflecting on *The Turtle Tattoo*, now approaching completion. Sitting in Nadine's apartment, I came to understand that no matter how important it was for me to write and publish this book, what I was doing at this moment was of equal, if not greater, importance. Slowly rising within me was the recognition that while the fulfillment of our personal dreams is critical to happiness, of equal importance is learning to balance our individual needs and dreams with the needs and dreams of others. A single strand, no matter how beautifully formed, is just a single strand. But a single strand connected to other strands, forms the amazingly complex, yet simple web that makes all life possible.

This insight, then, is the other secret destination I was meant to reach through writing this book—a task that forced me to grapple with the question of what brings happiness and what we must do to achieve it. These insights are the real gold revealed by the turtle tattoo—the gold that all the while was secretly shining in the dark, waiting for my discovery. It is my profound hope that your dream-realizing journeys will yield up equally rare and priceless treasure.

DREAM-REALIZING PRINCIPLES

- *Clearly identify a dream that mirrors your life purpose.*
- *Replace dream-defeating thoughts and beliefs with dream-supporting ones.*
- *Set concrete goals and persist until you have accomplished them.*
- *Have faith.*
- *Focus on one thing at a time; focus on what you must do to achieve lasting joy.*
- *Visualize your dream in strong and evocative imagery, and see it as if it already exists.*
- *Affirm your dream with colorful and emotionally charged words and speak as if it has already been realized.*
- *Express gratitude to those who help you, and be thankful for the riches you already possess.*
- *Be compassionate towards yourself and others.*
- *Act on the instructions given to you in night dreams and waking visions.*
- *Let go of your desire when the time is right.*

ABOUT THE AUTHOR

$\mathcal{M}$argaret Olivia Wolfson has been active in the fields of storytelling performance, writing, and aesthetic education for many years. In 1982, she received a Master's degree from New York University in mythic literature and performance, and subsequently founded *World Myth and Music,* a group devoted to the performance of mythic stories from world cultures.

Margaret has re-created a large body of tales and performed them, with musicians, for thousands of adult and young audiences throughout the United States and around the world. From 1986–1989, she wrote and performed her full evening-length Middle Eastern storytelling epic, *Majnun Layla,* with a musical ensemble and full scenic design, at many cultural and educational institutions, including a gala premiere at the Kennedy Center for the Performing Arts.

In 1991, Margaret was selected to be a U.S. representative in the New York International Festival of the Arts. She has been an ongoing performer and workshop leader, and has received many awards and honors for her outstanding contributions in the field of performing arts. She teaches workshops on storytelling as a fine art and the use of mythic stories as tools for personal transformation. She is also active in the area of curriculum design and teaching.

Margaret is the author of *Marriage of the Rain Goddess,* a full-color book for all ages.

For more information about her performances, lectures, seminars, consulting work, newsletter, and other activities, please call 1-800-595-5654.

ABOUT THE STORIES

*A*ll of the myths and folktales appearing in this book are my own, wholly original retellings. In most cases, my retellings have been based on numerous versions of the same tale. However, in a few cases, I based my retelling on only one main English source. I wish to extend my appreciation to the following authors, storytellers, and publishers who *first* made those public domain stories available to the general English-speaking public. These authors, storytellers, and publishers are:

Kirin Narayan, who collected a version of the story about the minister and the king (pages 38–39) from a holy man in western India. Her transcription of the holy man's telling is published in *Lives Stories Tell: Narrative and Dialogue in Education,* edited by Carol Witherell and Nel Noddings (New York: Teachers College Press, 1991).

Surya Das, who collected a version of the story about the man seeking enlightenment (pages 69–71) from a Tibetan monk, and retold it in his book of Tibetan folktales, *The Snow Leopard's Turquoise Mane: Wisdom Stories of Tibet* (New York: HarperCollins, 1992).

Diane Wolkstein, who collected the story about the man who would not listen to his dream (pages 103–104) from a Haitian student and retold it in her book *The Magic Orange Tree and Other Haitian Stories* (New York: Schoken Books, 1980).

Leila Fish, a member of the Hoh Tribe, who told a variant of the Native American folktale about the eagle's feather (pages 113–114). This story was collected by Steven Wall and Harvey Arden and published in their book *The Wisdomkeepers* (Oregon: Beyond Words, 1990).

Nataraj Publishing is committed to acting as a catalyst for change and transformation in the world by providing books and tapes on the leading edge in the fields of personal and social consciousness growth. *Nataraj* is a Sanskrit word referring to the dynamic, transformative power of the universe. For information on other books and tapes from Nataraj Publishing, please contact us at:

Nataraj Publishing
P.O. Box 2430
Mill Valley, CA 94942
(800) 949-1091